DATE DUE			
Apr 25 80			
GAYLORD M-2			PRINTED IN U.S.A.

THE UNDERTAKING /
Thief / The Pig

THE UNDERTAKING/
Thief/
The Pig

DAVID TRAINER

 **random house · new york**

To Lynn Fennerty

Contents

Introduction

The Undertaking was begun almost a year ago, and it has grown in pieces, slowly at first. It was originally a short play about two old people left in a deserted room with the body of a dead friend. I am not quite sure when this situation began to expand in my mind, but shortly after the one act was completed, I realized that there was much more to the play than I had written: the body was much more than that of a friend, it was a controlling factor in the old peoples' lives; it decreed their isolation and defined their existence. And strangely, the skeleton play attracted images, demanded company.

So very soon the first real draft of the present play was underway, and as I had suspected, the expanded story coalesced easily around the two old people, Alice and Claude. The original one act is now so hidden in the four subsequent drafts of the play that even I have trouble identifying it, but certain intentions have remained the same.

Perhaps it can be said that *Undertaking* concerns itself with definitions, and the clarification of these is its *intent*. And the primary definition involved is also the final one: death. It seems to me that the old people, with the help of Morris, have rationalized themselves out of an immediate confrontation with the cold death of a corpse.

They treat their corpses and their own assumed deaths with varying degrees of cordiality, as one would a houseguest one found somewhat less bothersome than the houseguest one had previously entertained. Of course this cordiality strains them a little, but as Claude points out, they have a sense of humor. Morris controls the deaths, and death controls the old people, and really it all works out rather well.

Peter however comes from a more absolute world, or at least a world more absolute than the one in the cellar. He is not prepared to deal with the fact that contradiction is as easy to live with as unity, especially if one is forced to. So he quite simply descends into the cellar without the preparation and acclimation afforded the rest of the group. And because death concerns him as much as it does anyone, he is driven on to experience it in all its privacy.

The action is simple. It is of consequence to Peter in particular, and the audience in general, if only because everybody dies *sometime*, and the experience must at least be a curious one. And the play is constantly shifting, moving out from under any preconceptions, *inducing* a sense of everybody "falling away," and leaving the viewer, like Peter, alone in a room as the light goes out at the end.

The response to this in the theatre was varied, to say the least. It is immensely difficult to categorize audiences, or what they do, and it is equally difficult to "answer" their questions. But I think *Undertaking* itself, the text, contains certain responses which may help. To those who say they don't care to see a play about death, Alice says, "You wouldn't have liked the country tree any better."

To those who ask what is wanted, Claude replies, "What do *you* want?" For those who wonder when an experience like this begins, Peter answers, "When I was younger . . ." And to those who ask why, Morris answers, "No reason. There's never a reason."

So during rehearsals for the first production of the play at The Playwrights Unit, the company took great care in discovering the intricacy of the web woven by Morris, and in defining the shifts which actually *necessitate* Peter's final statement. The text was left the job of telling *what happens*, and the actors placed the emphasis of their work on clarifying *how* it happens. Several points in particular relating to this process bear repeating.

Although the action of the play *can* be explained in logical terms, a fuller realization of Peter's predicament is arrived at if his role takes on certain emotional colorations as it goes along. Perhaps the closest analogy to this process is "lust." At first his mind is tantalized by the appearance of the old people, but later his physical desire to kill is exploited, and finally his compulsion to actually experience death. But this condition demands a certain kind of staging. Instead of shaping the play in great sweeps, the director, Chuck Gnys, built its reality from moment to moment, as it happened. Gnys drew on different aspects of the characters as those aspects became forces, and the actors responded *by way* of the text, not *because* of it. Perhaps what I am saying is that *The Undertaking* is a director's play, and an actor's play, and not a playwright's play. There is no imposed motivation. The action cannot be explained because "Morris is a bad guy," which he is not, or because "Peter is naïve," which he is not. It just, well . . . happens.

Neither *Thief* nor *The Pig* has been produced, so I can only say how they were written, not how they will eventually appear on stage.

There are three conditions which attended the beginning of *Thief*, and each was adjusted somewhat as it became part of the play.

I once saw a lady on the street who appeared to be the ugliest, most hideous woman on earth. And her sheer grotesqueness pulled me toward her as we walked along. But as I drew closer, I saw that she was also a hairsbreadth away from being the most beautiful woman on earth. In fact, she vacillated between the two extremes, and the vacillation accounted for her magnetism. She became Alice.

An actor once told me a story about a young lady of his acquaintance who was approached by a punky kid on the subway one night. He said he had a knife in his pocket, and would slice her up if she screamed. She began to talk, a constant stream of normal conversation, and kept it up to save her life. At the Museum of Natural History on Central Park West she got off the subway to go home, and the punk followed her. So she kept up the stream of chatter until she was right in front of the museum, a terrifying and imposingly dark building at night. She then turned and said quite simply, "If you put that knife away and leave me alone, I won't tell your mother. If you don't, I'll tell her what you've done." The boy was completely shaken, retreated a few steps, begged the girl not to tell, and disappeared into the night. The "mother" line went to Alice, and the punk became Rico.

A friend once told me how, at the age of fifteen, he was picked up by a prostitute. She kept making subtle propositions, but, misunderstanding, he responded to each with a naïve, cheery platitude. This continued for about a half an hour, and bit by bit he sensed that there was something strange about this woman. Finally the full implication of the conversation dawned on him, and in confusion, outrage and shame he stormed away. Implication became Alice's weapon, and confusion Rico's downfall.

The Pig is a short domestic horror story. It is for the reader, however, to discover the specific horrors, so I would rather consider the play in a technical way instead of impeding another's responses with my own.

The Pig's most important device is the compression of time. When performed, it will probably run for about a half an hour; it appears to be the action of a single evening. But I think it is in fact the relationship of three people over several years compressed *into* a half an hour. This telescoping brings a certain urgency, a certain immediacy to the play which could be expressed in no other way. And the relationship itself is not absolutely specific. So the play becomes the characters' moment-to-moment intimation of what happened through the years; for it is impossible to *know* what is *really* happening until *after* whole sections of time have elapsed. But there is no "afterward" for Michael, Mell and Cynthia. There are only the immediacies, the compression. I suppose that any sequence of events compressed in this way would become a horror story.

Undertaking, *Thief*, and *The Pig* belong together. Chronologically *Thief* came first, in the spring of 1967. The one act from which *Undertaking* derived was originally intended as *Thief*'s companion piece, as the two dealt very obliquely with the nature of invoking a sense of death. *The Pig* was finished in the spring of 1968. Technically it owes much to *Undertaking*, which was completed in the fall of 1967, because both demand in their own ways that the reality of the moment be established before the reality of the total play can exist.

So they are all together. And happy. And rightfully so.

David Trainer
New York City
April 11, 1968

THE UNDERTAKING

THE UNDERTAKING *was first presented by the Playwrights Unit, 15 Vandam Street, New York City, on April 4, 1968. It was directed by Charles Gnys. The cast, in order of appearance, was as follows:*

ALICE   Diana Webster
CLAUDE   Louis Beachner
MORRIS   Michael McCarthy
PETER   Jeremiah Sullivan

Production Manager   Mac McGinnes
Stage Manager   Lynne Prather
Designer   Robert Troie

SETTING:

An elevated passageway upstage from
which stairs descend to the stage floor;
the stage is perhaps a combination living
room-parlor, and is in any instance
rather drab; there are trap doors in the
floor which lead to a lower, unseen area.

TIME:

One afternoon to the next.

SCENE ONE

ALICE *enters from below. She pauses and returns to the trap door.*

ALICE Claude! Claude! (CLAUDE *appears, mumbling*) What have you got?

CLAUDE A question.

ALICE Oh yes? What?

CLAUDE (*Reading*) "Yesterday a Webb's Fort woman watched the second of her two sons die in two consecutive days at Regiment Hospital here, only to be revived by doctors at the clinic."

ALICE The woman or her sons?

CLAUDE Which. Exactly. That was my question. Who died and who was revived, and if it were the sons isn't it libel to refer to them as dead in the printed publications.

5

ALICE How old is that?

CLAUDE Recent.

ALICE *How old?*

CLAUDE Recent . . .

ALICE Where'd you get it? You've just layed hold of it. Where? (*Pause*) You've been reading that man, haven't you? Haven't you!

CLAUDE No.

ALICE You ripped it off that man . . . you plucked him, didn't you?

CLAUDE No.

ALICE Bastard. I say yes!

CLAUDE Now, now . . .

ALICE I said you bastard! You took it right out from under him, didn't you? You went downstairs, through the trap, and came back with that thing, that clipping, in your mitt . . . Morris will have your head for that! Well, there's only one assemblage of newspaper in this house and we both know where it is. We both know very well what purpose it serves. And we know it's for wrapping, not reading! I said we both know, don't we!

CLAUDE   No.

ALICE   What do you mean, no! You mean yes, I believe . . .

CLAUDE   I mean not necessarily. It might not be from the assemblage.

ALICE   But you've been reading that man, haven't you! You've been improving yourself on his poor body!

CLAUDE   No.

ALICE   Guilty!

CLAUDE   No!

ALICE   Of course you are. You've been down there with your flashlight reading away at that poor man, poring over the sports section and sucking up the socicty announcements. Will you save me the crossword next time you unravel one?

CLAUDE   I haven't been reading him.

ALICE   Well, don't! Morris doesn't read him. I don't read him. We get along fine. Why don't you try a little forebearance yourself!

CLAUDE   Enough . . .

ALICE   Tell me this though. Does he recommend the good articles? The interesting tidbits. Like, "Say, Claude, there's a nice note in real estate there . . . right. That's it . . . and it says rent on basement warehouse space is going up. Will my weekly portion be raised because of this notice?" Does he say things like that?

CLAUDE   No. He doesn't.

ALICE   Good. I wouldn't want him feeling too free with you . . . But I definitely think you two should remain friends . . . at any cost.

CLAUDE   We're friends.

ALICE   Good. Then be nice and don't read your friend's wrappings. Decent people place a limit on the bounds of friendship, you know. (*Pause*) How are you going to return the article which you may or may not have removed from your friend's assemblage?

CLAUDE   Have you got the tape?

ALICE   Downstairs in the drawer. (CLAUDE *exits*) But see, it's me who drives you to decisions, not yourself. Without my persuasion you might have left that man stripped. Remember that. And in the future try to display a better array of good judgment without my indicating the critical points. If that's at all possible.

CLAUDE   (*Offstage*) Yes. (ALICE *mutters incomprehensibly.* CLAUDE *reappears*) Done.

8

ALICE   Did you do it well?

CLAUDE   Done, I said.

ALICE   And did you do it well, I said. So as to conceal your blundering from Morris? Did you do it that well? (CLAUDE *descends again, and reappears*)

CLAUDE   Completely done.

ALICE   I should hope so.

CLAUDE   I don't see how I couldn't replace a short human-interest story in a newspaper with a piece of tape.

ALICE   You went back down to check . . .

CLAUDE   "Always check your work." I've always done that.

ALICE   That's admirable. From private enterprise?

CLAUDE   Yes it is.

ALICE   Why were you fired? Because you died?

CLAUDE   Shut up!

ALICE   Private enterprise and you parted ways. Remember?

CLAUDE   I don't remember . . .

9

ALICE   Perhaps you will elsewhere.

CLAUDE   Where else?

ALICE   In an insane asylum.

CLAUDE   Pardon?

ALICE   I said you might like it better in an insane asylum!

CLAUDE   Oh . . . no thank you.

ALICE   Yes.

CLAUDE   I don't think so.

ALICE   Why not?

CLAUDE   I don't care for the name.

ALICE   What would you like it to be?

CLAUDE   Home. I'd like it a home.

ALICE   You've got a home. Why not an insane asylum!

CLAUDE   The name makes my skin crawl.

ALICE   Where do you suppose the place is?

CLAUDE   Which?

ALICE   The insane asylum.

CLAUDE   In the country. Outside the city. Morris would know.

ALICE   I'm asking you.

CLAUDE   It's a large, very obscure address. Very obscure. I'm never sure where it is.

ALICE   Have you looked?

CLAUDE   No.

ALICE   Oh yes you have.

CLAUDE   No!

ALICE   I thought you'd want to know where Morris and I are going to put you. I'd think you'd be very interested. It'll be your *home*.

CLAUDE   I don't know where it is. I don't want to know. I've looked, I can't find it. I don't want to look any more.

ALICE   Go on.

CLAUDE   When I was younger . . . I looked. They wouldn't say. No one would say. No one would tell me where.

ALICE   How do you know it's in the country?

CLAUDE   It would have to be. There'd be a lawn there, and a tree . . .

ALICE   You never asked correctly and you haven't the faintest idea what to expect. You might enjoy it. Morris and I would.

CLAUDE   What?

ALICE   Morris and I would enjoy seeing you enjoy it.

CLAUDE   It's large, very obscure. In the country outside the city. Very hard to discover the directions. When I was younger . . .

ALICE   Why is that?

CLAUDE   It is, that's all.

ALICE   You don't want to know. You never asked properly, you never asked so someone would tell you, and then you go around saying you can't find things exactly.

CLAUDE   I spent a whole day looking.

ALICE   One day from a lifetime. From two lifetimes! That's nothing. Not even asking the right questions. That's magnificent. You're a magnificent specimen. When you get there—in the country—they'll be over-joyed. And Morris and I will put a little tag around your neck giving the pertinent information: "Hullo. My name is Claude. I'm here for a bit and my problem is, though I'm a fine workman and an admirable man about the house, I don't know how to ask proper directions in a simple straightforward fashion. So I'm here because my two previous keepers, the undersigned, went out and sweat blood to find this rotten stinking lawn with this one tree for me to rest under. So while I'm here, feed me, clothe me, kiss me, wrap me up, and if I get killed in the electric shock room don't mind too terribly because I'm a stinking foul old man who can't hold his head up outdoors! . . . Thank you and God bless you, signed," and so on and so forth. That's what we'll hang around your neck.

(*There is a pause*)

CLAUDE Where's Morris?

ALICE Out.
(*Another pause*)

CLAUDE You're a bad wife.

ALICE I'm not your wife. Remember that. We live together, but marriage is too far. You're unquestionably lower-class material out of which to make a husband. (CLAUDE *hisses*) We ought to consider another room. Perhaps only temporary.

CLAUDE Why temporary? We should expand. Build up!

ALICE It wouldn't need to be permanent, Claude.

CLAUDE Why not?

ALICE   Because it would be for you, and you're not permanent. You're headed for that lawn with the tree. And I'm not sleeping with a madman any longer.

CLAUDE   Why not?

ALICE   Last night you wet the bed in your dreams.

CLAUDE   I didn't dream last night.

ALICE   But you wet the bed, and that was it!

CLAUDE   Where would you sleep?

ALICE   Alone. In my own bed.

CLAUDE   I don't believe you.

ALICE   You don't have to. Just remember: inferior, lower-class material shows. And you show all over the place.

CLAUDE   You wouldn't do that.

ALICE   Yes I would. Wait and see.

CLAUDE   You know this makes you live-in help . . .

ALICE   No it doesn't. It relegates you from artificial husband to second-rate boarder. Transient. On route to your tree. So keep that in mind as you snooze tonight. You're one step closer to your tree. You're one step closer to insanity. You're one step closer to being dead!

(*There is a pause.* MORRIS *enters along the passage-way. He wears various articles of black clothing. He descends, and then disappears through the trap doors. Another pause*)

MORRIS (*Offstage*) Who's been reading this man down here!

Blackout

MORRIS *and* ALICE *are sitting with a glass of something each.* CLAUDE *hovers behind, waiting table.*

MORRIS   Well, Dad?

ALICE   He's not your Dad any more.

MORRIS   Is Alice telling the truth, Dad?

ALICE   Of course I am. I'm your mother.

MORRIS   Then you won't be sleeping down the hole any more, Dad? It'll be just us three now?

ALICE   That's right.

MORRIS   Alice. Shut up.

ALICE   Claude, go down and wash the glasses. Get out of my sight.

MORRIS   Come on.

ALICE   He's a fool.

MORRIS   Is that right, Dad? Are you a fool?

ALICE   He's a madman.

MORRIS   That too, Dad?

ALICE   A maniac.

MORRIS   Well?

ALICE   A lunatic.

MORRIS   Eh?

ALICE   All those things.

MORRIS   All those things, Dad? Are you?

CLAUDE   No.

MORRIS   He says he's not.

ALICE   Go wash the glasses.

CLAUDE   I'm still waiting table.

MORRIS   That's right, Alice. He's still waiting table and
there's no reason he should have to pick up something
else before this job's done.

CLAUDE   I'm conscientious.

MORRIS   That's admirable. Alice, you go wash the glasses.
Now get on it!
(*There is a pause.* ALICE *rises and descends through
the trap doors with the glasses. Another pause*)

CLAUDE   Black, eh? . . .

MORRIS   Black's very good right now. I'm into another
pile . . . at least I will be pretty soon. These are just
my size.

CLAUDE   Oh. Do we have this old black much longer?

MORRIS   I doubt it. Not if this new black comes through.
We'll need space.

CLAUDE   There's that. Alice has me moved up here
though.

MORRIS   So I've heard.

CLAUDE   But I'll never do it. I'll be down there again tonight.

MORRIS   Will she mind?

CLAUDE   She won't remember. Who's the new black?

MORRIS   Friend of ours. You'll be happy to see him again.
He's invited by for later this evening, but just to chat.
That's all I want for tonight. Just a chat.

CLAUDE   Bit of fooling?

MORRIS   Maybe. Be good for him.

CLAUDE   I've got some ideas . . .

MORRIS   Surprise me.

CLAUDE   If Alice goes along with it. She's bad today.

MORRIS   Yes. Well. The bitch.

CLAUDE   She does all right though, sometimes.

MORRIS   Yes.

CLAUDE   But she doesn't understand what you're up to. She thinks things come from nowhere, or if not from nowhere then from places where she's got complete control. She's got to choose one or the other. Can't have both. Either nowhere or somewhere. Then she'd understand what you're up to.

MORRIS   You could give her lessons.

CLAUDE   Yes. I could.

MORRIS   Why don't you?

CLAUDE   Well . . .

MORRIS   Why not?

CLAUDE   She's too dumb. I think that's it.

MORRIS   That would be a stumbling block.

CLAUDE   Too dumb and stupid is the answer.

MORRIS   Could be.

CLAUDE   Definitely.

MORRIS   Hmm.
          (*There is a pause*)

CLAUDE   Have you heard her mention a tree?

MORRIS   Tree?

CLAUDE   Yes. And a lawn. She's got a fixation.

MORRIS   Tree and a lawn?

CLAUDE   Fixed firmly in her stupidity.

MORRIS   With what other words does this fixation mani-
          fest itself?

CLAUDE   Other words.

MORRIS   Which ones?

CLAUDE   I don't remember.

MORRIS   I can't help you then. I've got to have a context.

CLAUDE   In the context of the country then.

MORRIS   Like nation?

CLAUDE   No. Country as opposed to city. That context.

MORRIS   Is that all?

CLAUDE   I can't remember. No. An address too.

MORRIS   I can't say I've noticed that fixation.

CLAUDE   Oh. She says it's a creation of yours.

MORRIS   Well, I've been busy with the blacks lately, Dad.

CLAUDE   No recall of it then?

MORRIS   Not in this form. But I'll keep it in mind.

CLAUDE   Yes. Do that. (*He pauses*) Do you think we need another room?

MORRIS   We need a lot of things, but I hadn't thought of another room.

CLAUDE Never thought of another room?

MORRIS Has this got anything to do with the tree and the lawn in the country?

CLAUDE Not directly, no.

MORRIS Indirectly then?

CLAUDE I don't know.

MORRIS Well, then *I* don't know. Another room'd be nice.

CLAUDE What could we use it for? For instance.

MORRIS I don't know ...

CLAUDE Yes. Well keep all this in mind.

MORRIS Sure. (*He pauses*) Why not go off now, Dad? Get ready and all. Take a nap.

CLAUDE Yes. I'll do that.
        (*There is a pause*)

MORRIS And don't worry. I'll keep all this in mind.

CLAUDE No.

(*Pause.* CLAUDE *descends through the trap doors.* ALICE *appears through the trap doors*)

ALICE   Visitors, eh?

MORRIS   Another black.

ALICE   You got any requests?

MORRIS   Behave. We're just talking tonight.

ALICE   Just talk?

MORRIS   He's an old friend of ours. I want to study the hang of his blacks before I get into anything.

ALICE   And you want us?

MORRIS   Dad knows.

ALICE   You're in black yourself.

MORRIS   Well, not completely. Style is black.

ALICE   Black's quite a thing now.

MORRIS   A trend.

ALICE   And you like it?

MORRIS   It's a trend. (*He pauses*) What's Dad doing downstairs?

ALICE   Napping, he says.

MORRIS   Why would he do that?

ALICE   He's not well. Maniacal, you know. He is.

MORRIS   No.

ALICE   Yes. He is. Stark-raving maniac. The raving tires him out. Being a maniac takes energy. Insanity encompasses all the bodily functions as well as the mental ones.

MORRIS   That's why he's resting?

ALICE   Yes.
   (*There is a pause*)

MORRIS   Have you heard him mention a tree?

ALICE   A tree?

MORRIS   And a lawn. Tree and a lawn.

ALICE   No. How would he know about trees and lawns? He wouldn't.

MORRIS   And an address. In the country.

ALICE   I don't remember . . .

MORRIS   Oh.

ALICE Why?

MORRIS He was onto me about it. Said it was your conception. I told him I hadn't heard a word. Had no conception of the whole business.

ALICE Oh.

MORRIS Where would he get a thing like a tree and a lawn and a country address?

ALICE I don't know. The raving's worse some days than others. Sometimes when you're out it gets very bad. And he has trouble in his sleep.

MORRIS What?

ALICE Well, dreams. And emissions of various sorts. That sort of thing. His mind's become very fertile. It lunges and consumes things, and several days later they reappear at the surface in the form of something stupid. And he raves some. That's the process, I think.

MORRIS Hmm.

ALICE So I wouldn't worry. He's just losing his mind. That's all.

MORRIS Well, I'm reassured then.

ALICE Yes. Rest assured.
        (*There is a pause*)

MORRIS   Well, get ready. The black'll be here in a bit and you should both be ready. Give us time though.

ALICE   Yes.
(*A pause.* ALICE *descends through the trap doors. Blackout*)

SCENE THREE

MORRIS *and* PETER, *a minister, enter along the passage-way.*

MORRIS   Here we are.

PETER   I see.

MORRIS   I can't offer you anything.

PETER   Words are more interesting than food anyway.

MORRIS   Yes. Sit down.

PETER   I haven't been here in some time.

MORRIS   No?

PETER   Not since before your parents died.

MORRIS   I believe you.

PETER   It isn't changed any.

MORRIS   Oh, some. Perhaps some. Things unnoticeable, you know.

PETER   Oh.

MORRIS   Well, I'll tell you why I had you over, you see, that being the fairest way.

PETER   Yes.

MORRIS   If you can't talk to your clergyman, after all . . . Well, you are my clergyman, aren't you? I mean, you are clergy and your church is nearby and my parents, when they felt up to it, the trip and all, the bowing and scraping, they went to your church around the corner, so I supposed you were still my clergyman.

PETER   Yes. I am.

MORRIS   Well, that being the case, I wanted to talk to you for lack of anyone else. (*He pauses*) I've got a question. It's for someone I know. The answer is—if there is an answer—that remains to be seen, doesn't it? . . . This person talks constantly of some place, some location where there's a tree set out on a large lawn of green grass, and this setting strikes him as right for an insane asylum. He wants to go there. He's buggered about going, in fact. He adores the place. But . . . he doesn't know where it is, and when he goes around searching he claims he can't find it. Now I'd ordinarily help him, be of assistance, but my mind runs in other directions than insanity. So the man is left alone and

must do the looking himself. But . . . and here's another thing . . . he doesn't ask the directions in such a way as to get an answer. He runs around mouthing the problem, but never gives anyone the information necessary to help him. He says, "It's a large, very obscure place, in the country, outside the city, very difficult to discover . . ." But he never gets any closer than that. (*He pauses again*) Now what we'd all like to know is: in your opinion is this man a psychopath of some sort?
(*There is another pause*)

PETER Why?

MORRIS Because he appears to be, doesn't he?

PETER Not necessarily.

MORRIS Of course not that. But probably is what I'm asking, not necessarily. He's probably a psychopath, isn't he?

PETER What can I say?

MORRIS Yes or no. Or maybe. Or that you aren't qualified to answer objectively. You can say almost anything and get away with it.

PETER I can't answer. I can't judge.

MORRIS Oh. Then we'll have to let it go, won't we? Let it ride.

PETER   Yes. (*He pauses*) Now I have a question for you. You see I came quite readily tonight because I had a question for you.

MORRIS   What? You did what?

PETER   I came quite readily because I had a question for you.

MORRIS   You mean you wouldn't have come readily on my account alone? You rely upon your own curiosity to dictate whom you visit and whom you don't? You're saying that's your discrimination process?

PETER ' No.

MORRIS   What are you saying?

PETER   That I was ready to come, that's all.

MORRIS   Oh. Well then. I misunderstood.

PETER   But in the death of your parents . . .

MORRIS   In what?

PETER   The death of your parents . . . what again were the reasons?

MORRIS   Wet lights . . .

PETER   What?

MORRIS   Your eyes are like wet lights dripping into some
stone burial ditch. (*He pauses*) They expired due to an
overdose of electrical current coursing through their
individual bodies. Death was instantaneous. Death by
power line. Now why do you want to know?

PETER   There's no record of their burial.

MORRIS   Ghoul!

PETER   There isn't any record . . . I was never called for
a service. I wondered . . .

MORRIS   I took them to their old country home, where
they could lie beneath the moon and stars in their old
country homeground. Now you know.

PETER   I wondered. I never heard anything after the
deaths were announced.

MORRIS   They're dead. Both of them. Both dead. (*He
pauses*) So those are the facts. (*He pauses again*) Now
there's that *address* in the country . . . rather difficult
to come by. That faraway address of a place equipped
only with a lawn and a tree and this unknown address.

PETER   For your friend . . . I've already said . . .

MORRIS   Yes. I know.

PETER   I don't know.

MORRIS   You've never heard of this place?

31

PETER   No.

MORRIS   Absolutely no recall?

PETER   What do they do there?

MORRIS   It's a resting place. They say the tree grows nicely because of the surroundings.

PETER   No I tell you.

MORRIS   Oh.

PETER   Why do you want to know? What's the significance? What's the value of knowing? Will the answer serve any worthwhile purpose? Perhaps the proprietors of the address don't want you to discover it. Perhaps they prefer anonymity. Perhaps they're secretive about the activity there. Perhaps the tree's symbolic. Perhaps there is no such place. All those things. You have to take into account other people's wishes. I think I detect explicit wishes in the secretiveness of the address.

MORRIS   And you don't know who *they are. It* is. *The* tree.

PETER   Absolutely not.

MORRIS   I don't believe you. (*He pauses.* ALICE *and* CLAUDE *are heard, unintelligibly, below*) Oh. My . . . guests.

PETER   I thought we were alone. I didn't know there were others.

MORRIS Let me introduce you . . .

PETER You never warned me. (ALICE *and* CLAUDE *appear through the traps; they are dressed very elegantly in black dinner clothes*)

MORRIS Mr. and Mrs. Bouchet . . . The Very Reverend—

PETER Just Reverend.

MORRIS The Just Reverend . . .

ALICE How do you do?

CLAUDE Charmed, I'm sure. Peter?

MORRIS Yes. Reverend Peter . . .

PETER How do you do?

MORRIS From France, Peter. Bouchet. It's a French name. Across the sea.

PETER Yes. I see.

CLAUDE Reverend?

ALICE Are you of God? By that I mean of course are you one of His people? In His employ?

CLAUDE Reverend?

MORRIS Reverend . . . the Just Reverend Peter.

PETER Yes.

CLAUDE   Then you're a minister?

PETER   Yes.

MORRIS   Starchy white collar and all, Mr. Bouchet. See for yourself. (*To* PETER) French, you see.

ALICE   He's very absent-minded, Peter. You must forgive him.

MORRIS   French.

PETER   I see.

ALICE   How very nice of you.
      (*There is a pause*)

MORRIS   Peter here and I were just discussing the untimely death of my beloved parents.

PETER   No we weren't.

MORRIS   Yes we were, Reverend.

CLAUDE   I knew them well.

ALICE   Damn shame.

CLAUDE   Very well, in fact. Studied with old Claude in Paris. But that of course was before he died.

MORRIS   Of course.

ALICE   He was an old bastard, if you ask me.

PETER   Madame!

ALICE   You don't think so?

PETER   I certainly believe—

ALICE   He was an old bastard.

CLAUDE   Who was?

ALICE   Claude was. Dear.

CLAUDE   Now about those clothes you're wearing, Reverend . . .

MORRIS   Ah ahh. No, no, Mr. Bouchet.

CLAUDE   What?

MORRIS   We're not going to talk about Reverend's clothes. Are we?

ALICE   No.

CLAUDE   Oh no.

MORRIS   You're damned right you're not!
         (*There is a pause*)

PETER   Well, I—

ALICE Well nothing. Sit down. Relax. We want to get to know you.

CLAUDE Yes. I'd like to ask you some things.

ALICE Shut up.

MORRIS Mr. Bouchet, I suggest you rest your mouth a while.

CLAUDE What?

ALICE You heard him. Now, Reverend . . .

MORRIS Are your parents dead?

PETER Yes.

MORRIS Can you prove it? I mean, I never received an invitation to the groundbreaking. As a matter of fact, I never saw anything in the paper. I wasn't notified. I have only your word on it.

PETER Yes. That's all you have.

MORRIS Your word's not official. It's not even sanctioned. It's practically hearsay.

PETER Not to me.

MORRIS But you're dealing with me. Me. I've got to know too. It's public information, yet you consistently obscure the facts. Now tell me. Are your parents dead?

PETER   Yes. They are.

MORRIS   At the time of my parents' departure I was very shaken . . .

PETER   I can understand.

MORRIS   Shut up. (*He pauses*) After . . . it . . . I was driving back here. I had a few relics: a pocket watch, my aunt, two cousins, a cat, a press-clipping book related to the deaths, and a pair of shoes. And it was a borrowed car. We were speeding along a very dusty, winding, backwoods road. I decided suicide, or some variation upon that theme, would be an appropriate gesture. So I edged toward the side—we were going eighty-five— and began to examine the passing trees for a suitable resting place . . . There were plenty of easy shots. But there was nothing I liked. Nothing attractive enough to do. And the more I examined the trees as they shot by, the more I realized that, should I commit suicide in a speeding auto carrying not only myself but a great deal more in the way of useless fat, baggage, reminiscence, et cetera, I would be mitigating the tragedy of my own departure. The sadness of my death would be alleviated by the cheer of all theirs. And there were three people other than my living self in that vehicle. Do you see my problem? Three departures of no consequence to one departure of sensibility and strength. I was on the losing end three to one. The suicide was futile I realized. I couldn't die. I was restricted to life. So while debating this circumstance I drove two wheels off the road, into the forest, and left two wheels rolling in the dust. I hoped a misplaced tree might hit the car and kill all but myself who, as you see, was unfortunately immune at the time. Well, nothing happened. No stray trees, not even a stray branch. I must have stayed half on, half off the road for hours. Nothing . . . I saved those lives out of kindness.

PETER   I have to go.

ALICE   No you don't. You can't.

PETER   I have work . . .

CLAUDE   Work? At what?

MORRIS   Man of God, Mr. Bouchet. Reverend Father. He's with the church, the house of God around the bend.

CLAUDE   Ah ha.

ALICE   Idiot.

CLAUDE   Yes . . . I never noticed your suiting. Now I see. You are with God.

PETER   Yes.

ALICE   In His employ, Father.

CLAUDE   Then there's a church nearby. God's domicile. His hut hereabouts. Yes?

38

ALICE We've been harping on that a little recently, Father. You didn't hear?

CLAUDE No. I certainly didn't. Well, tell me, are there services?

PETER Sunday mornings.

CLAUDE One or two?

PETER Two.

CLAUDE Do you fill up both, or is there a seat for sale before the curtain?

PETER There are seats.

CLAUDE What, isn't it a good show?

PETER There aren't enough people in the neighborhood to fill two services, but there are too many for one.

CLAUDE Is there singing?

PETER Yes. Hymns.

CLAUDE Is there dancing?

PETER No.

CLAUDE No dancing at all?

PETER No. It's frowned upon.

ALICE I'd imagine.

CLAUDE I wouldn't. I can't believe that. Singing, but no dancing. He's telling me they charge full price for half a show. Are there lightworks and tumblers? Matmen and weight lifters? Bareback horses and trapeze ladies? Vaudeville bits? Blackface routines? Banjo pickers? Guitarists? Fat ladies? Midgets? Anything like that?

PETER Nothing. Just the straight service.

CLAUDE That's all? Not even a dwarf?

PETER No.

CLAUDE Then you'll have to come do a private service here and we'll give you decent equipment. I can't imagine a show without entertainment.

PETER It's a very conservative church.

CLAUDE I'd say so. I may have to come see for myself.

ALICE Don't be a fool.

CLAUDE Yes. Perhaps you're right. Without dancing I'd get depressed. I won't come after all.

PETER You'll be welcome if you change your mind.

ALICE Of course he would. Mr. Bouchet gets into the finest places in the world. I'm sure he'd be welcome in your church.

CLAUDE   So you are, in effect, a minister.

PETER   Yes.

CLAUDE   Well, I'll think it over. That's all I can promise.

PETER   Do. Ours is a very warm congregation.
     (*There is a pause*)

MORRIS   Reverend. These people could help you in the area of our previous discussion: the area of my parents' demise and departure unto the dead and whatnot.

PETER   We never discussed that.

MORRIS   Perhaps. But if you're interested anyway you might talk to them.

CLAUDE   Indeed.

ALICE   Alice and Claude. Fine people. Noble, you know. Aristocratic to the bone. A fine gentlelady and superb idiot.

CLAUDE   A magnificent couple . . . but with a sense of humor. A mighty and fierce spirit Claude was, and a tremendous fine bitch Alice.

ALICE   It's too bad the way they went.

CLAUDE   Claude was a brave man . . .

ALICE   There was a duel . . . they shot each other. The blow from Alice's bullet knocked Claude off an elevated field into a network of high-voltage wires. He was burnt unrecognizable.

CLAUDE   Electrocuted. Alice was so mad she took her own life rather than be without Claude. She dove immediately into the wires.

ALICE   There on the field of honor . . .

PETER   We've never discussed this before.

MORRIS   Perhaps not. But it's fun. They had a flair for that sort of thing.

PETER   And they are dead?

ALICE   And buried.

CLAUDE   And rightfully so. (*He pauses*) But you're a minister, correct?

PETER   Yes.

CLAUDE   Well, you should know then. You know about dead people . . . you know what happens to them and where they go and all. That's your business. Isn't that your business?

PETER   Only partially.

ALICE   What's the other part?

PETER   I can't say.

ALICE Oh.

MORRIS Well, I'm not certain about that.

PETER I am. I can't.

MORRIS Isn't the other part about the living, whatever that may be?

PETER I'm not committed.

MORRIS I can imagine that.

PETER The dead or the living. No matter. It's secret business, all of it. People are lucky enough to get into church to see the surface. It's the business beneath the surface that's important, so the people will never know.

CLAUDE Pity.

PETER No it isn't. They wouldn't understand.

CLAUDE They can't understand the surface without dancing!

MORRIS Shut up! You old fool! (*He pauses*) Excuse me.

PETER Of course. Mr. Bouchet, you expressed an interest in my habit a while ago. Do you like it?

CLAUDE Yes. Yes I like it. I'm interested.

PETER Feel it if you wish.

43

CLAUDE It's very soft, isn't it?

PETER See for yourself.

CLAUDE I do see.

MORRIS What the Reverend means, Mr. Bouchet, is that you should feel absolutely unrestrained in making an inspection. Go ahead.

CLAUDE I know what it's like.

ALICE You most certainly do not.

CLAUDE I do. I don't need to touch.

PETER You'll like it.

CLAUDE I know. I don't need to touch.

PETER There are thousands of threads in this suit. Millions. Yet to make a fabric, some of the strands—about half—must go across the others, be woven against each other. The result is the cloth I wear. If you touch it you'll hold a physical representation of contradiction. Yet the suit isn't contradiction at all, but a unity. (*He pauses*) It's not often you'll get an offer like this.

CLAUDE No.

MORRIS You've never received an offer like this before, Mr. Bouchet.

ALICE   The Reverend is giving you something, Father. Thank him.

CLAUDE   I haven't received it yet, you know.

PETER   We're waiting.

MORRIS   Go on. We're waiting.
(PETER *removes his jacket and holds it out to* CLAUDE. *There is a pause.* CLAUDE *takes it*)

PETER   Now give me yours.

CLAUDE   What?

MORRIS   You heard him, old man. Give him your jacket. This has to be a fair deal.

PETER   I can't go about half undressed, can I?

CLAUDE   That wasn't mentioned.

MORRIS   No, but give it to him anyway. He's naked.

ALICE   Father, you're foolish. You can't ask a man to go around without a coat. Give it to him.

CLAUDE   I won't wear this unless I get the collar and front too.

PETER   Fine.
(PETER *removes his collar and front*)

45

ALICE   But that's another bargain, Father. You'll have to give up your ruffles now. And your studs.

CLAUDE   No.

MORRIS   Yes. What do you think this is? Give up your vestiges. Hand over your frills. You don't need that trash.

PETER   Here's my front. Now yours, please.

CLAUDE   No.

PETER   Yours, please. I'm afraid I can't take no for an answer.

CLAUDE   No.

PETER   Mr. Bouchet . . . (PETER *grabs* MR. BOUCHET— CLAUDE—*by the throat, violently*) Give me that shirt or I'll break your neck!

ALICE   Good.

CLAUDE   But—

PETER   The shirt and tie or your neck!

CLAUDE   Let go!

PETER   Will you take it off?

CLAUDE   Yes.

PETER   Then take it off. All of it! I want all of it! (PETER *frees* CLAUDE) There. Off with it.

CLAUDE   Will I like the clothes?

MORRIS   When you get that frill off you can see for yourself.
        (CLAUDE *removes his dress shirt and bow tie*)

PETER   That's better. Don't you feel better already?

CLAUDE   I don't know.

ALICE   You will soon enough though, won't you, Father?

PETER   Now put on that black front and collar. Come on. We want a display of reverendsmanship. Button up. Good fit?

CLAUDE   It'll do.

ALICE   Is that all? It's beautiful on you, Father, you know.

PETER   God's smiling.

CLAUDE   I'm not.

PETER   God's chuckling.

CLAUDE   I don't like it.

PETER   God's laughing hysterically.

CLAUDE   I hate this.

PETER   I said, God's laughing hysterically!

CLAUDE   And I'm not!

PETER   What? You'd better laugh, boy. Laugh good. Laugh hysterically. Remember you're one of God's boys now, and when He laughs, you laugh. When He cries, you little boys cry too. Understand.

CLAUDE   Yes.

MORRIS   Well, laugh then. You heard him—laugh!

CLAUDE   I can't.
        (PETER *pushes* CLAUDE)

PETER   You damn well better.
        (CLAUDE *starts, feebly*)

ALICE   Harder, Father. I don't think that's enough.

MORRIS   Harder!
        (PETER *pushes* CLAUDE *again*)

PETER   Laugh harder! Laugh until you bleed! Laugh! Laugh! Laugh!

MORRIS   You're snickering.

ALICE   More, Father, more.
         (CLAUDE *is now in hysterics*)

PETER   There. Now that's laughing. (*He pauses*) You're
getting there, Mr. Bouchet. Don't ever forget that.
You're just getting there.

CLAUDE   Give me my frills.

PETER   No. A deal's a deal. You can even have dancing
now, though don't expect to get approval.

CLAUDE   I want my clothes back.

PETER   You've got your clothes on. Reverend.

MORRIS   Enjoy them, Mr. Bouchet. Travel freely in them.

PETER   I'm rather enjoying these.

CLAUDE   You bastards.

MORRIS   Tut tut. None of that.

ALICE   You look fine, Father. Give us a spin around the
room so we can soak in all the grandeur.

CLAUDE   No.

PETER   Oh, Mr. Bouchet. You can't refuse . . .

CLAUDE   What?

MORRIS   You heard him. Give us a spin, Mr. Bouchet. The Reverend Mr. Bouchet.
   (PETER *pushes* CLAUDE *away*)

PETER   Get spinning.
   (CLAUDE *begins to spin around and promenade*)

ALICE   More graceful. You don't inspire anything that way.

MORRIS   More rhythm.
   (CLAUDE *stops his promenade*)

CLAUDE   Shut up!

PETER   Now, Mr. Bouchet . . . Perhaps you need a prayer to play with. Come here.

ALICE   Yes. I'm sure of that. He must need a prayer.

PETER   I'll give you one, Mr. Bouchet. Something you'll find terribly useful as one of His boys.

CLAUDE   No.

MORRIS   Yes. You need one. You'll like it.

CLAUDE   These clothes itch.

PETER   He's after you already? It must be because you
haven't prayed yet. Come here. We'll get right to it.
(CLAUDE *goes to him*)

CLAUDE   No.

PETER   Yes, Reverend. Sit down . . . yes, right here. Are
you relaxed?

CLAUDE   No.

PETER   Fine. One should be very tense when one prays.
And you're going to pray.
(*Everyone remains absolutely still*)

CLAUDE   No.

PETER   Repeat after me: When the beginning is reached . . .

CLAUDE   When the beginning is reached . . .

PETER   And the voice is very soft . . .
(MORRIS *moves slowly to the passageway*)

CLAUDE   And the voice is very soft . . .

PETER   There is the simple assimilation.

CLAUDE   There is the simple assimilation.

PETER   There is no more one, but many ones in a greater
thing . . .

CLAUDE   There is no more one, but many ones in a greater thing . . .

PETER   A mass consisting of one.

CLAUDE   A mass consisting of one.
(MORRIS *disappears*)

PETER   And the one grows until at last there is little to do but die.

CLAUDE   And the one grows until at last there is little to do but die.

PETER   Making space. Space means liberation.

CLAUDE   Making space. Space means liberation.

PETER   And there are so many liberations.

CLAUDE   And there are so many liberations.

PETER   There is little that can be done, little to change the procedure.

CLAUDE   There is little that can be done, little to change the procedure.

PETER   Is there an answer?
(*There is a pause*)

CLAUDE   Is there an answer?

PETER   There is the simplest answer to all the requests . . .

CLAUDE   There is the simplest answer to all the requests . . .
(MORRIS *enters along the elevated passageway. He
carries a potted tree. He stops at the stairs*)

MORRIS   Mr. Bouchet! For you!

Blackout

CLAUDE *is seated and chained to the tree; he still wears the clerical collar.* ALICE *enters from below, to water the tree.*

CLAUDE   What's he going to do with me?

ALICE   Shut up.

CLAUDE   You've got no right to chain me.

ALICE   You've got your tree now. You've been looking all over for a tree and here it is, and now you've got it you want to know what else is coming. Shut up.

CLAUDE   This isn't the right tree.

ALICE   A tree, any tree for you, Claude. That's a fine tree. Maybe it isn't the address you wanted, but it's still a tree.

CLAUDE   It won't do without a lawn.

ALICE   There's no lawn here.

CLAUDE That's what I mean. This won't do at all.

ALICE Shut up.

CLAUDE That address . . . wouldn't be like this. It would be in the country, with another tree, and a lawn. Not like this. Something better. This is squalid—squalid!

ALICE Keep shouting and Morris'll hang you.

CLAUDE You wouldn't let him.

ALICE He can do what he wants. I don't care.

CLAUDE Where is he? Did he kill Peter?

ALICE *You've* got the blacks.

CLAUDE I'm chained!

ALICE Morris knows.

CLAUDE I won't agree to anything.

ALICE You old fool. Mr. Bouchet won't agree to anything, but old Claude wants to save his neck.

CLAUDE This isn't the right tree.

ALICE You wouldn't have liked the country tree any better. You'd have been just as lunatic there as you are here.

CLAUDE I wouldn't. I'm not lunatic.

ALICE We say you're lunatic. Peter knew it the minute he saw you. Written all over your face. Maniacal, raving, lunatic: pathological tendencies.

CLAUDE Let me go.

ALICE No.

CLAUDE Let me go! We've been married! This is grounds for action, you know.

ALICE You'll rot at that tree.

CLAUDE When I'm loose you're dead, understand? I'll wring your neck.

ALICE You'll never be loose.

CLAUDE We'll see.

ALICE Shut up.

CLAUDE You're dead.

ALICE I find myself very much alive and breathing.

CLAUDE Bury yourself.

ALICE I'm busy.

CLAUDE   Mortified, that's what you are.

ALICE   And you.

CLAUDE   *Iieeee!* Ghoul! Witch! Dead woman! Get away!
Go! Damn dead don't touch me!

ALICE   Enough! Enough, you maniac! (*She beats him
with a towel, violently*) Stop! Stop! Stop!
(PETER *and* MORRIS *appear through the trap doors;*
ALICE *stops without noticing them*)

ALICE   Never say that again! Hear me? Don't speak!

MORRIS   Is the prisoner acting up?

ALICE   He's a maniac!

MORRIS   Which is why he's chained. Don't worry. He's
got his tree . . . and his lawn, such as it is. He's happy.
Aren't you, Mr. Bouchet? I mean, you are happy, aren't
you?

CLAUDE   Yes. I'm happy.

MORRIS   See? No need to be violent. He's a happy lunatic.
How's the tree?

CLAUDE   Lovely.

MORRIS   I'm glad you like it. I chose it with you in mind.

ALICE It should be bigger, stronger.

MORRIS He won't escape.

ALICE It should be much stronger. I don't trust that tree.

CLAUDE It'll do fine. I'm getting to like it.

MORRIS I hoped you would.

CLAUDE It's a very fine piece of tree, all things considered.

MORRIS Well, hang on.
        (MORRIS *disappears through the trap doors*)

CLAUDE (*Whispering*) Ghost! I see a ghost! Out of the grave!

ALICE Shut up!

CLAUDE Dead! I see the dead creeping all over you, tiny little deads! (*Covering his eyes*) Save me from the sight!

ALICE (*Leaning over him; in his face*) Claude! You're mad, insane! Stop it, I tell you! (*She grabs a long kitchen knife, and holds it to him*) I'll slit your throat if you don't stop! Cut out your guts! Stop it!
        (*Silence;* CLAUDE *uncovers his eyes*)

PETER You'd better behave.

CLAUDE   Sorry, Reverend.

PETER   I'm not the Reverend any more. You're the Reverend. Look at your collar. Let's have no more mistakes like that. We must know ourselves, mustn't we?

CLAUDE   Sorry.

ALICE   He's maniacal. When do we do him?

PETER   Do him?

ALICE   Run him through.

PETER   Run him through?

ALICE   Hang him. (*She pauses*) I don't like lunatics chained up in my parlor.

CLAUDE   And they don't like being here!

ALICE   Madman!
      (*She descends through the trap doors*)

PETER   There's a dead man in the cellar. Did you know that? Wrapped in newspaper.

CLAUDE   No.

PETER   Yes. Morris showed me.

CLAUDE   No he didn't.

PETER   I saw the body. (*He pauses*) She wants to kill you, you know. And then wrap you in newspaper, just like the other. (CLAUDE *hisses*) I knew old Claude . . . and Alice . . .

CLAUDE   Good.

PETER   I'd see them. They came to church. They were around, and I certainly knew them.

CLAUDE   What do you want?

PETER   You can tell me. I want to . . . straighten things out. You can tell me things because I know better. I go through things.

CLAUDE   Go through hell.

PETER   This is a house of murderers. You're part of it, part of the house. You can tell me, because I knew old Claude . . . and Alice . . . And I won't leave.

CLAUDE   Morris! Morris!

PETER   Shut up! Tell me.

CLAUDE   Ghoul . . .

PETER   Perhaps.

CLAUDE   You damn fiend!

PETER   Shut up, old man. You haven't got much time to be calling names.
(MORRIS *appears from below*)

CLAUDE   Let me go.

PETER   Not a chance.

CLAUDE   When I get loose I'll kill you.

PETER   Hardly.

CLAUDE   Slit your throat.

PETER   No.

CLAUDE   You're dead!

PETER   No, Mr. Bouchet. *I* am immune to superstition. *You're* the dead man, and have been so for quite some time I'd imagine. You and that charming little lady. Don't try to scare me please. It won't work.
(PETER *exits through the trap door*)

MORRIS   You've been hollering, haven't you?

CLAUDE   Yes. What'll you do with me?

MORRIS   What'll you do with yourself, you mean? Now that you've got your lovely tree.

CLAUDE   That man's a fiend, Morris. I tell you he's a fiend.

MORRIS   Which man?

CLAUDE   That Peter, fool. That preacher.

MORRIS   You're the preacher, old man.

CLAUDE   *Peter,* I tell you. The ghoul. He knows! He's seen the boarder and he knows. He'll kill us, Morris, if you don't get him. He knows.

MORRIS   You're dead already.
      (*There is a pause*)

CLAUDE   You're taking him in. Opening up. You'll give us all away. What's doing this?

MORRIS   I've had the call, Claude.

CLAUDE   You have not, you bastard.

MORRIS   I've seen the light.

CLAUDE   You're blind.

MORRIS   I've awakened to life.

CLAUDE   You're a filthy killer and you know it!

MORRIS   I'd watch that, Claude.

CLAUDE   Will you kill me? Have you got *me* chained up to kill? Have you?

MORRIS   You're lunatic, Claude. You've been lunatic since the wire burning, since the old char session. You've been out of your skull. I don't worry about you dead or alive. You're worse than dead.

CLAUDE   I can speak.

MORRIS   Drivel.

CLAUDE   You're a stinking bastard.

MORRIS   Every day you spend out looking for that address. You come home and whine away the nights rumbling to yourself and drooling about some faraway tree until you can go out and look again. Well, now you've got your tree. Be happy. It's all that's in it for you, old man. All you get when you're dead.
   (CLAUDE *hisses*)

CLAUDE   Vermin! Stinking vermin!

MORRIS   Drivel.
   (ALICE *appears through the trap door*)

CLAUDE   (*Covering his eyes and shaking*) Death! Foul death! A ghoul!

ALICE   Shut up, shut up, shut up! You damned old man! You stinking maniac! Insane! Insane! Insane!

63

MORRIS   Stop it.

ALICE   You've got to do away with him. I can't live with that chained beast in my house! Kill him, I tell you! Kill *him*!

MORRIS   He's already dead. You know that.

ALICE   Nobody's dead. Before, a simple dead man was enough. You've got the collar you want. Do something. Kill *somebody*. (*She pauses*) Show me something, Morris. Show me something!
   (*There is a long pause.* MORRIS *exits through the trap door*)

CLAUDE   Help me. Tell me something! Help me!

ALICE   I don't even see you.

Blackout

CLAUDE *is at the tree.* MORRIS *and* PETER *enter from below.*

PETER   There's a kingdom for the dead, Morris.

MORRIS   Have you been thinking about that? About telling me? I know.

PETER   Not here, not in the cellar . . .

MORRIS   I know.
(MORRIS *quickly ties a black hood over* CLAUDE's *head*)

PETER   You're a killer.

MORRIS   No I'm not.

PETER   There's a man dead. Wrapped in newspaper.

MORRIS   I didn't do it.

PETER   Did you know him?

MORRIS   Mildly. He stinks now. Smell him?

PETER   Did you know him?

MORRIS   Mildly.

PETER   You knew him and you killed him.

MORRIS   Knowing doesn't mean that.

PETER   Why?

MORRIS   I liked his clothes. I've got them on; these, well, not all of these. The shoes aren't his.

PETER   You killed him for his clothes and wrapped him in newspaper. When?

MORRIS   I didn't. The old people wrapped him. I didn't kill him.

PETER   You and the old people.

MORRIS   Mr. and Mrs. Bouchet. The French.

PETER   Of course.

MORRIS   I'm glad you see it that way. Reverend.

PETER   I'm not a Reverend. There's the old man. Look at his neck. I'm not the Reverend.

MORRIS I know.

PETER Why'd you do it?

MORRIS No reason. There's never a reason. I just didn't.

PETER How many are there?

MORRIS How many do you want? How many should there be?

PETER Would you kill me a man? Do it for me?

MORRIS I'd kill you one. But you'll do it better. After a while.
 (*He pauses*)

PETER I was a Reverend.

MORRIS You came in one. I know.

PETER You're a murderer. A filthy killer.

MORRIS I don't like that.

PETER Killer. (*He pauses*) Clothes killer. That's all. I was a reverend and you . . .

MORRIS You want one all for yourself. One man.

PETER   The church . . . my church . . . That this exists, that—

MORRIS   You know it. And you can't go back, really. Not now that you know how much more there is.

PETER   There's a kingdom of them . . .

MORRIS   Without any reasons, Reverend.

PETER   I'm not that. Not that! Look at him!
(ALICE *appears from below; she carries a black cape, and mounts the stairs to the passageway; she waits by the exit*)

MORRIS   I'll get you one . . . for all you know. You'll wait?
(MORRIS *mounts the stairs to the passageway and goes to* ALICE. *He puts on the black cape and exits to the outside. There is a long pause.* ALICE *descends from the passageway and gives* CLAUDE *a swift kick as she passes*)

ALICE   He's off.

PETER   Hunting.

ALICE   Yes.

PETER   Does he always go dressed like that?

ALICE   Mostly. He's got lightweight gear for summer.
(*She pauses*) He says he likes the ancient look of the

stuff. I think he took it off a foreigner. (*About* CLAUDE)
Quite peaceful, isn't he?

PETER   He's a very peaceful old man.

ALICE   He's maniacal, you know.

PETER   I hadn't noticed.

ALICE   Yes. Very much. We'd never have him out of our
sights for fear he'd rig some apparatus.

PETER   Apparatus?

ALICE   Some hanging or knifing or something. It was
always on his mind, plain as day. Turn your back and
he'd be fiddling with string and scissors. Never trust the
maniacal.

PETER   Yes.

ALICE   So we planned to put him off. But now he's got
what he was after. He was always after a tree, you see.

PETER   Was he?

ALICE   Yes. He had a tree perversion. Always wanted to
be chained to a tree. This one's quite nice, I think.
Everyone should have a tree.

PETER   Yes.

ALICE Well, he's a lunatic and maniacal, so watch yourself.

PETER Of course.

ALICE Don't ever let him behind you.

PETER No.

ALICE Don't ever give him string or scissors.

PETER Certainly not.

ALICE And kill him first chance you get.

PETER What?

ALICE Kill him. Do him out of his misery. You know. Stop him for good.

PETER He's chained.

ALICE No matter. Remember: he's lunatic, stark-raving mad.

CLAUDE A dead woman! Spiders, creeping animals! The flesh! Crawling, peeling back, flaking blood! Save me from the pallid woman!

PETER Mr. Bouchet.

CLAUDE Look out, Reverend! She's death! She'll be after you straight off. Beware. Beware!

PETER I'm beyond that sort of thing.

ALICE You stinking old man!

CLAUDE Beware! Beware!

PETER Shut up!
(*There is a pause.* CLAUDE *hisses*)

ALICE Reverend.

PETER I'm not the Reverend. He is. Look at his collar.

ALICE Whatever you are. Now you've seen it! He's maniacal!

PETER I don't know. I merely object to the volume, not the content.

ALICE He's lunatic.

PETER Perhaps.
(ALICE *moves to the trap*)

ALICE Beware. Both of you!
(*She descends*)

PETER   Mr. Bouchet.

CLAUDE   You kicked me. Why was I kicked? I'm chained. I'm hooded. I shouldn't be kicked too.

PETER   Yes.

CLAUDE   Listen Peter. Peter is your name, isn't it? Yes. Now listen Peter—just unchain me and we'll discuss this unnecessary kicking. (PETER *removes the black hood*) Why did you kick me?

PETER   I didn't.

CLAUDE   Yes you did.
            (*There is a pause*)

PETER   I'm afraid it was Morris.

CLAUDE   You liar. He wouldn't do a thing like that.

PETER   He did it.

CLAUDE   Liar. You kicked me while I'm chained. Kicking a chained man. That's miserable. That's akin to sin.

PETER   Don't talk to me about sin.

CLAUDE   Liar—liar—Liar!

PETER   Once more . . .

CLAUDE   Once more what, Mr. Peter? Once more what? Kicking a chained man. Brutal.

PETER   (*Standing directly above* CLAUDE)   Listen, Claude.

CLAUDE   I'm not Claude!

PETER   Claude.

CLAUDE   You're wrong, I tell you! I'm not Claude!

PETER   Claude.

CLAUDE   That was Morris' father. He's dead. Gone. Buried. He's away with the dead. You're wrong!

PETER   Claude. (*He pauses*) Claude, you're a filthy dead man. Do you understand? Dead! Now you might be other things too. You might be a maniac. Lunatic. Morris' father returned in the shape of a lunatic. Something like that. A very subtle little arrangement in your imagination. What is it, eh, Claude? What is it?

CLAUDE   Not Claude.

PETER   In any instance it's Claude. Any possible combination or arrangement and your name's Claude. Now what are you. Lunatic?

CLAUDE   Sane.

73

PETER   Dead?

CLAUDE   Alive.

PETER   Then there's going to be a change.

Blackout

PETER *is seated.* MORRIS *comes through the passageway as he departed.* CLAUDE *sits at his tree.*

MORRIS   Damn.

PETER   What?

MORRIS   Nothing.

PETER   What?

MORRIS   Empty. They're empty.

PETER   What's empty?

MORRIS   The streets. Not a soul on the streets. I walked for miles.

PETER   You didn't.

MORRIS   I say I did. Not a soul. Not a single body. Not a person. Not an arm or a leg or anything. No eyes. No mouths. Nothing.

PETER What are you saying?

MORRIS There's nothing.

PETER No bodies? Not a one? I thought you were good at this.

MORRIS I am.

PETER It doesn't appear so. Why not?

MORRIS There wasn't anything. Not a soul.

PETER There are always people out.

MORRIS Not this time.

PETER Liar. They just weren't your size, were they?

MORRIS Nobody.

PETER Too tall or too short or too fat or too skinny. That's it, isn't it?

MORRIS No.

PETER Vain. You're vain, that's what you are.

MORRIS Go out and look for yourself.

PETER   I don't have to.

MORRIS   Go on. Nobody out there. They're all away somewhere.

PETER   Liar!

MORRIS   Go on. I told you. Go see for yourself. Blank
streets, empty pavements, the whole thing. Go on. Look!

CLAUDE   Maybe they've all gone for a holiday in the
country.

PETER   No.
   (*He pauses*)

CLAUDE   Just as I thought—no bodies.

MORRIS   Keep still.

CLAUDE   You were banking on one, weren't you?

MORRIS   Shut up.

CLAUDE   Not a soul on the street, eh? Off in the country,
I suspect. That's my belief. Off in the country.

PETER   Old man . . .

CLAUDE   I was counting on this all along. So now you
can unchain me. Let's go.

MORRIS   No.

CLAUDE   Morris!

PETER   (*Standing above* CLAUDE)   Old man . . . Mr.
Bouchet . . . consider yourself . . . it. Once dead . . . as
good as dead twice.

CLAUDE   The chains.

MORRIS   No.

PETER   You've been designated, old man.

CLAUDE   What?

PETER   Morris is going to kill you.
        (*He pauses*)

CLAUDE   I haven't been to the country . . .

PETER   Don't simper.

MORRIS   It's really better this way.

CLAUDE   I don't think so! I'm not ready . . .

PETER   You've had more than enough time I'd say.

CLAUDE   I'm not prepared!

PETER But it's too late now, isn't it?

CLAUDE Bastards.

PETER Now now . . .

CLAUDE Bastards!

MORRIS I don't want you to die upset.

CLAUDE I don't want to die at all . . .

PETER Strange words from a deceased.

CLAUDE I'm alive.

PETER Sorry. I read it in the paper. You're dead.

CLAUDE I have to go to the country . . . there, I have to feel home somewhere . . . there, there's an address which would take me in, a lawn, they have a tree . . .

MORRIS You have your own tree now.

CLAUDE There are other people, others, they're the same . . . They feel the same . . . weary, they sleep and sit and it's calmer, less frantic, less pressure there . . . there is an address, a careful address, a secret address, how do I get there? How do I? Yes. You. You. How, how? Where is it? I've looked. I have looked and wandered

79

and it never comes, everybody disappears, everybody falls away, and there's no address which can be discovered ... there ... there ... there ...
(CLAUDE *bows his head as if in sleep*)

MORRIS   He's gone.

PETER   Kill him. Do it.

MORRIS   Not yet.

PETER   Get it over.

MORRIS   He's sleeping. He's passed by us.

PETER   Do it for me.

MORRIS   You'll do it better.

PETER   I was a Reverend!

MORRIS   You came in one. I know.

PETER   You're a murderer. A filthy killer!

MORRIS   Clothes killer. That's all.

PETER   The church ... my church ... That this exists, that ...

MORRIS   You can't go back. Not now that you know.
(*There is a pause.* ALICE *appears through the trap door*)

ALICE   Get anybody, Morris?

MORRIS   One.

ALICE   What's he got on?

MORRIS   What?

ALICE   What's he wearing?
(*There is a pause*)

PETER   Black.
(*Another pause*)

ALICE   Tell me, Peter . . . Reverend Peter. When?
(*A pause again*)

PETER   When I was younger, before . . . I don't know exactly . . . I would be struck by the urge to escape. And I would find safety in books, vast piles of fine literature, bound in the finest leather and inscribed with the finest inks. I would gather a large selection and lock myself in a room with only a bed. Then I began. I read. (*He pauses*) You see, I have a fine memory. I can recall everything I've read, in every detail. I can recreate whole books from memory. Perfect recall. (*He pauses*) Once I had set myself apart with the books, I didn't plan to leave the room until I'd read them all. Every single one. I had a single purpose. (*He pauses*) I had a small room, very dark and secluded. There was no chance of interruption. I was alone. And I began to read. I remember the time very clearly. Perfectly. There were marvelous books. The twenty finest books ever written. And I was reading them: avidly. (*Another pause*) At the seventh book my mind began to slow, slacken. Everything slowed to an excruciating pace. Heavily. And it would take an hour to turn a page, a year to complete a chapter. My whole body spun, lost itself in the spinning. I was lost. And it was ecstasy. (*He pauses.* ALICE *mounts the stairs and exits along the passageway*) I remained in this state for several books. I don't know how long. I had no way of telling time other than by volume, volume by volume, page after page, a word at a time . . . By letter. (*He pauses again.* CLAUDE *begins to undo his chains*) At the fourteenth book I became aware of a new stimulus: my own personal odor began to permeate, to creep into my universe. And the odor grew in pungency, magnified itself in the stillness of the room until it was the prime force. The odor destroyed as it grew, until there was only the odor. (*He pauses.* CLAUDE *mounts to the passageway and exits.* MORRIS *follows slowly*) I finished the twenty books. Though my memory is perfect I cannot remember the last six. They were lost in the odor, in the pungency of my existence in the room. As I put down the final volume I fell asleep . . . a heavy state, drugged. I slept endlessly until at last I awoke, thoughtlessly, bathed myself, dressed and left the room to rejoin the world as I had previously known it. (*He pauses again.* MORRIS, *at the exit, disappears. Another pause.* PETER *is alone*)

Morris! Come back! Morris, bring them back! They're dead, you said so. Dead and insane! (*Another pause*) At least leave me Claude! Let me have the old man! I'll kill him! He won't feel it! It won't hurt! Morris, give me that man! I'll kill him! (*He pauses*) I'll kill myself.

Blackout

THIEF

Characters

RICO:
A tough kid of about twenty.

ALICE:
A well-preserved woman of fifty.

SETTING:

The living room of an old apartment.

TIME:

The present.

The scene is in the living room of an old apartment, well furnished though certain incongruities are obvious, i.e., several ornate chairs are set around, yet among them is one absurdly ugly, stiff, white, chipped wooden chair. There is a couch at stage right running from upstage to downstage; some tables covered with porcelain figures are set opposite the couch. A hall to the bedroom is up right, and a hall to the front door is up left. The openings to the halls are extremely shadowy. There is no window.

As the lights rise a creaking, prying sound may be heard. There is a sudden snap! RICO *has broken in the front door. The door opens and almost immediately he appears at the entrance to the hall, stealthily.* RICO *wears stiff new blue jeans, scuffy black shoes, a tee shirt and a shabby rain jacket. He has black hair trimmed short and long sideburns. He is about twenty. In his hand is a long stiletto knife, and in his belt a crowbar.*

He creeps cautiously into the room, staying against the upstage wall. As he reaches the dark hall to the bedroom, ALICE *appears suddenly, as if materializing out of the shadow.*

ALICE *is a woman of fifty years, somehow well preserved but in some certain way also hideous. She is proportioned strangely and is overly made-up. She wears a dark skirt, billowy blouse and slippers. She moves without a sound. As she steps out of the hall,* RICO *starts and then steps behind her, holding the stiletto in her back. Her expression doesn't change, though she stops walking immediately.*

RICO (*Nervously*)   Don't. Don't open your mouth.
    (*He moves to her side*)

ALICE (*Moves to the couch, where she lights a cigarette*)
    Good afternoon.

RICO (*Taking her arm*)   Sit down. Don't move.

ALICE   All right.

RICO   I said shut up. I mean it. Shut up.

ALICE   All right.

RICO   Who else is there?

ALICE   Who?

RICO   You heard me. Who else?

ALICE   Does your mother know you're out?

RICO   Shut up.

ALICE   Doing this? I don't even know you.

RICO   Lady, I got a knife.

ALICE   Do you mind if I smoke?

RICO   Lady.

ALICE   Alice.

RICO   Lady. You stay put. You move and you're dead, hear me?
        (*He disappears into the bedroom hall and returns almost immediately*)

ALICE   Anybody there?

RICO   No.

ALICE   There wasn't when I left. When I heard the door.

RICO   Are there any other rooms?

ALICE   You were pretty noisy. Not very good.

RICO   (*Projecting the knife*)   Any other rooms I said.

ALICE   Just two. Two rooms.

RICO   Kitchen?

ALICE   I order in. A refrigerator though, in the bedroom.

RICO   Don't talk. I wouldn't.

ALICE   You're not. Beer?

RICO   Shut up.

ALICE   Milk maybe?

RICO   Lady.

ALICE   Sit down, why not?

RICO   Lady. I got the knife.

ALICE   I won't force you.

RICO   You won't force me anything. Now shut up. I don't
want to kill you.

ALICE   Thank you.

RICO   I don't.

ALICE   And I said thank you. That's nice.

RICO   I have a knife. I might have to.

ALICE   I doubt it.

RICO   Don't be so wise, lady. Don't be a cute old lady or
I slit you wide open. I mean that, because I have a

knife, and I know what to do with it. I ain't kidding one bit.

ALICE   I haven't accused you of kidding. Don't be defensive.

RICO   You're going to be defensive in a minute if you don't watch out.

ALICE   Fine. Now sit down, why not? Be comfortable.

RICO   Where is it?

ALICE   Sit down. Where's what?

RICO   Whatever there is. Jewels. You know.

ALICE   Sit down. I'm sorry. My transactions are in cash. No jewels.

RICO   Cash then.

ALICE   Please sit down. Sorry again. No business today. The banks are closed. I have only a little cash, but you're welcome to it.

RICO   Get it—don't move. I'll get it. Where?

ALICE   I forget where I put my purse. I'll find it in a bit. Why don't you make yourself comfortable? Does your mother know you're here?

RICO   The cash, lady.

ALICE   In good time.

RICO   (*Amused, finally sits*)   Lady, you don't seem to see this shiv.

ALICE   It's nice of you to sit.

RICO   I ain't got all day. I'll have to cut you wide open if you just don't go get that cash.

ALICE   You'll have to be tougher. Snotty little punk. Pimply punk.

RICO   Lady, are you crazy? I got a knife.

ALICE   You are sweet.

RICO   Lady!

ALICE   Alice. I'm Alice.

RICO   Fine. Alice. The dough.

ALICE   Find it. (RICO *gets up, rummages about, always with one eye on* ALICE) What's your name? What do they call you?

RICO   Don't move, lady.

ALICE   Alice. I'm Alice.

RICO   Okay, now where is it?

ALICE   Is this your first job? I'm sure you've worked . . . you've got rough hands . . . but I mean job.

RICO   What?

ALICE   Job. Have you been in this kind of thing before? I doubt it.

RICO   I have a knife.

ALICE   Bully. You're a big pimple. Can I help you?

RICO (*Starting*)   Don't move. I'll find it.

ALICE   You're getting colder.

RICO   Shut up.

ALICE   No self-respecting thief does all this work. It's your first job. Isn't it?

RICO (*Sitting*)   Lady. First, I have a knife. Second, I'll cut your noisy throat. Third, you're so ugly it wouldn't make any difference. Now would you like to discuss?

95

ALICE   You're a cute pimple. Would you like a cigarette?

RICO   No.

ALICE   (*Going to him*)   Here. I'll light it for you. (*She holds out a cigarette and lights it for him. She returns to her seat*) You look more comfortable.

RICO   Well now. Maybe I do. Where is it?

ALICE   The cash?

RICO   Yeah.

ALICE   Finders keepers. Look around. You were getting a little warmer. I've traveled, you know.

RICO   Lady.

ALICE   I've been here and there.

RICO   You should watch your mouth. You should shut up more. You could get killed. I could kill you. I would. When I find that money I will.

ALICE   Yes. I'm waiting.

RICO   You wait. You'll see.

ALICE   First you're defensive. Then you threaten.

RICO   Yeah.

ALICE   I've been to South America.

RICO   You'll never get back.

ALICE   I don't want to go back. I've been.

RICO   You never will. You'll bleed to death.

ALICE   Pity. I like the tropics. There's snow there. On the mountains. You can see it from the jungle. I was with a pilot.

RICO   Yeah. And soon you'll be dead like him. The cash.

ALICE   Come on. Loosen up. It's early.

RICO (*Darts up and frantically starts to look for the money*) Where is it, where is it!

ALICE   You haven't looked in the other room.

RICO (*Picks up a piece of pottery from the table*)   What's this?

ALICE   A present. From South America.

RICO (*Smashes it to the floor*)   Not any more.
        (*He goes into the bedroom hall and disappears. He*

is heard rummaging about in the bedroom. ALICE
goes to the hall and calls after him)

ALICE   Find it? (*She pauses*) Want some help?
(*She too disappears into the hall. Almost immediately* RICO *returns*)

RICO   It's not in there.

ALICE (*Reappearing*)   I told you there was no one there.
There's only two rooms. You should have gotten a beer
while you were at the icebox.

RICO (*Sitting*)   Where is it? I don't like this.

ALICE   I'll tell you when you get near.

RICO   So those are from South America. That shit.

ALICE   Not all. Other places too.

RICO   What a happy little home.

ALICE   Shall I get you a beer?

RICO   Why not.
(ALICE *disappears and returns almost immediately*)

ALICE   In a glass?

RICO   The cash, lady. No jewels, so cash. Get it. No more of this noise. Get the money. I have a knife.

ALICE   You showed me.

RICO   Then get the money.

ALICE   (*Going to the stiff wooden chair*)   This belonged to my sister. She wasn't well.

RICO   Run in the family?

ALICE   My stepsister. Are you a nigger? Secretly?

RICO   (*Going to the stiff wooden chair. He kicks off one of the legs*)   Too bad about your sister. No.

ALICE   (*Returns to the seat*)   I thought you were. I thought you looked like one. But you're not.

RICO   I could cut your throat now. Not wait. Alice.

ALICE   I'm glad you called me that. Do get comfortable.

RICO   You're not helping any. The cash. Where's your purse?

ALICE   Sit down, why not? (*She rises and goes to the bedroom.* RICO *sits. She returns with a beer, in the can*) It's an aluminum can. They taste better. You won't mind.

RICO (*Takes a sip*) Is that the truth . . . (*He pours a bit on the rug*) This is a nice place.

ALICE I'm glad you're glad.

RICO Where's the money?

ALICE You keep asking. I won't tell. You have to look. You must know I won't tell you. The thief has to look. Pimple.

RICO (*Goes to the pottery and pours some beer on the figures; he places the can among the figures and returns to his seat*) Did I get it with the beer?

ALICE I'll tell you.

RICO Get it and then tell me. Then I'll cut your throat.

ALICE Are you short on cash? I could lend you a bit, you know. Pay me when you can.

RICO Get that money. I'll break things if I look.

ALICE Just sit and think about it. You speak nicely for whatever you are. A pimple. You must be short on cash. Short on something. Financially. (*She pauses*) You wouldn't buy beer. I'll give you all you want. Free. It must be something else.

RICO Time.

ALICE   A girl? A nigger girl. But you're not a nigger. But a girl.

RICO   Time is almost up. I'm going to cut your hairy throat.

ALICE   Does your mother know you're here?

RICO   No more noise. No more. You're going to be dead before your time.

ALICE   Simple pimple.

RICO   There's no window in this room.

ALICE   In the bedroom. There's one there.

RICO   Two doors but no window.

ALICE   Cozy.

RICO   Your purse, Alice.

ALICE   Why?

RICO   I'll kill you.

ALICE   Is this your first job?

RICO   I'll use this knife.

ALICE   It must be.

RICO   Cut your neck.

ALICE   Simple pimple.

RICO   Slit you wide open.

ALICE   You're getting colder.

RICO   Like flyboy. Your pilot.

ALICE   Does your mother know you're here? If I were your mother, I'd want to know where you were. You're a nice-looking boy.

RICO   What about my mother?

ALICE   Just asking. Don't get upset. I don't think your mother and I'd get along.

RICO   What about her?

ALICE   I don't think she knows what she's got.

RICO   You got some cash.

ALICE   Strapping. That's you. A strapping pimple.

RICO   Yeah?

ALICE   A tiny strapping pimple titmouse.

RICO You'll meet my mother. She's killed in a crash.

ALICE She couldn't serve you.

RICO You can get your cash for me.

ALICE She wouldn't sit you down and get you a beer.
And stroke you.

RICO How do you know?

ALICE I can tell.

RICO Perhaps you should just find the cash.

ALICE There go your fancy words again—"perhaps."

RICO Maybe I'm just going to kill you.

ALICE No torture. No rape.

RICO I have a knife.

ALICE (*Rising and going to the pottery*) See this? (*She
picks up a figure*) From China. Seldom one finds china
from China. (*She holds it over* RICO) See it? (*She holds
it against his head*) Hear it? (*She drops it in his lap*)
Feel it. Go ahead. You'll like it.

RICO It's nice.

ALICE   I hate it. You can have it. An anniversary present.

RICO   What?

ALICE   Anniversary. Your first job.

RICO   The cash! Get your purse. I won't sit here much longer.

ALICE   The couch is made of silk. Raw. The covering. Inside is hay. I looked. Too bad your mother doesn't know you're here. I hate her.

RICO   Shut up about her!

ALICE   She's insufficient.

RICO   I said clam up on her!

ALICE   Do I look like her? She had fat thighs though.

RICO   You have a hairy face.

ALICE   But she had thighs that slapped together when she walked.
(ALICE *turns and goes into the bedroom. A long pause*)

RICO   Get out of there!

ALICE   (*Reappearing*)   I thought I had her picture. I don't. I thought we did. From Easter.

RICO   Don't talk that. Shut up. Get the cash. I want to get out of here. I'm not sitting any more.

ALICE   You're the thief. I don't even know you. I thought we had a picture. Of your mother. The one with the fat thighs?

RICO   Shut up.

ALICE   But perhaps not. Maybe just you.

RICO   What do you mean?

ALICE   Maybe just a picture of you. At Niagara Falls. Remember?

RICO   I don't know who you are.

ALICE   You'll remember the picture. It was good. You were younger. It was after something.

RICO   What? After what?

ALICE   I don't know you. After something. I can't remember. Your mother should be here. She could look for the money while you chat. She'd remember. She might have been there.

RICO   Where! Now get the money. Get it! No more talk. I can't stand this talk!

ALICE   Yes. She was there. That's why I hate her. She shouldn't have been there. It was none of her business.

RICO   Shut up about my mother. Shut up about her!

ALICE   She's dead. Don't worry. Have you been in the army?

RICO   What?

ALICE   The army. Fighting.

RICO   No.

ALICE   Couldn't get in?

RICO   They didn't call.

ALICE   Too bad. You were lucky. I liked the army.

RICO   You weren't in the army.

ALICE   In South America I was with an army.

RICO   With flyboy.

ALICE   There are other armies than America's. I've worked with a few. Your country probably has one. Check on it.

RICO   My army would be here.

ALICE   Then the navy.

RICO   American army.

ALICE   I believe you. Even if you don't look it.

RICO   What's that supposed to mean?

ALICE   Nothing. You identify too strongly.

RICO   Get the money.

ALICE   No. Not yet. I don't get many callers.

RICO   I don't like that couch.

ALICE   Good. Sit on it. Go ahead. You'd look good in a uniform.

RICO   What?

ALICE   The couch has mahogany legs. Ugly dead wood.

RICO   I'll break something.

ALICE   I'll stand. Do you work alone?

RICO   What's that mean?

ALICE   Without accomplices. A gang. I thought all you pimply little kids had gangs. Are they outside?

RICO   Look and see.

ALICE   There's no window in the room.

RICO   In the bedroom.

ALICE   You look and tell me.

RICO   I'm not getting up until you get the cash.

ALICE   That's fair.

RICO   Fair don't count. Get it.

ALICE   Bully. Assert yourself. You like the couch.

RICO   Where's the couch from? South Pole?

ALICE   Are you tough?

RICO   I have a knife.

ALICE   Very good. You could move in if you want. I wouldn't mind.

RICO   There's only one bedroom.

ALICE   We could work something out.

RICO   I have a house.

ALICE   In the slums? Are you a slum child?

RICO   I'm here now.

ALICE   Good again. I think I'm stronger than you. I played baseball.

RICO (*Amused*)   What?

ALICE   Baseball. I played outfield.

RICO   In South America?

ALICE   In South America. Actually softball. There's a difference.

RICO   I hate games.

ALICE   Then you draw. Pictures. Words on walls.

RICO   Maybe pictures.

ALICE (*Motioning to the picture on the wall*)   Do you like that?

RICO   No.

ALICE   It's a print. I like it. Someone chose it.

RICO   It's lousy.

ALICE   If there were a window here, the curtains would have to match.

RICO   Yeah.

ALICE   You understand. There's so few men who do.

RICO   I know what you mean, if that's what you mean.

ALICE   You could pick the curtains. If there were a window. I could pick the wallpaper. You don't like baseball.

RICO   Games.

ALICE   Games. It'd look nice.

RICO   I suppose.

ALICE   But you paint. Draw?

RICO   Sketch.

ALICE   What?

RICO   Things. You know.

ALICE   No.

RICO   Whatever there is.

ALICE   That's a print.

RICO   It stinks.

ALICE   You're ugly. Pimple. What have you sketched?

RICO   Things around.

ALICE   Any good?

RICO   I don't know.

ALICE   You could sketch here. When you move in.

RICO   No light. There's no window.

ALICE   I could see what you do. You could sketch me.

RICO   You're ugly.

ALICE   You could sketch me. Someone did that once.

RICO   In South America?

ALICE   I can't remember. A woman. Someone bought it.

RICO   It probably stank.

ALICE   I was naked.

RICO   You have fat thighs.

ALICE   Someone bought it. You could sketch me. A woman did it. I'd be the model and you'd be the artist.

RICO   Sure.

ALICE   When you move in.

RICO   I'm not moving in. Get the money.

ALICE   Don't push. Not yet.

RICO   I have this goddam knife.

ALICE   If I were your mother I'd want to know where you were. You're a nice-looking boy. You'd be amusing to have around. Your mother should know where you are.

RICO   Get the cash.

ALICE   Before you wanted jewels. You sort of lighten a room.

RICO   There's no window here.

ALICE   Sort of brighten a place. That's something. But your mother is dead. Right?

RICO   Shut up.

ALICE   Yes, of course. Just checking.

RICO   Shut up on that.

ALICE   Of course. Do you like the couch? (*He gets up*) Did you?

RICO   No.

ALICE   There's hay inside. I checked.

RICO   I have a knife.

ALICE   I checked with a knife. Stuck it in. Play with the china.

RICO   I'll break it all. Smash it.

ALICE   If you like.

RICO   I don't like all this shit all over the place. This place is a mess. You should do something about that. Really. Who lives in a hole like this? You should do something about it.

ALICE   You live in the slums.

RICO   All this china shit.

ALICE   Presents. Nothing. Break it.

RICO   This place is a mess.

ALICE   Did you go to school? Do you?

RICO   What?

ALICE   I'd have sent you to a good school.

RICO   Shut up.

ALICE   Better than you must have gone to.

RICO   What do you mean?

ALICE   You speak nicely. Someone taught you. I'd have seen that you were taught better.

RICO   I want the money.

ALICE   You've no education. Educated people don't talk about money.

RICO   No? Well get it.

ALICE   It would have been a private school. There you wouldn't have been bothered.

RICO   Nothing bothers me.

ALICE   I would have said that you were some kind of imported noble. No one would have guessed.

RICO   Nice pottery.

ALICE   And before that you'd have gone to some lovely day school. Not the church though. Better. And even before that a nursery. There you'd have made the right connections.

RICO   No.

ALICE   You're a nice-looking boy. It would have worked well. I knew you could do anything.

RICO   Yes. I can.

ALICE   I knew it when I sent you. Everyone said that
when they saw your baby pictures. You'd wear a nice
pair of shoes.

RICO   I went to school.

ALICE   I know. We had fun. Remember how I'd walk you
across the street? . . . the large street. The one you
were afraid to cross.

RICO   Lady, I don't know who you are.

ALICE   The teacher was very fond of you. The teachers.
You were contagious.

RICO   Nice picture. Nice couch.

ALICE   Relax. Let an old woman remember.

RICO   No.

ALICE   Is this your first job?

RICO   No.

ALICE   It must be. Pimple. Too loud coming in. Too
stupid to find the jewels. It is the jewels you want, isn't
it? Pimple.

RICO   No, lady. Your cash. Remember? I'd get it. I've got
a knife. I'm going to slit you open.

115

ALICE   Pimple. You're still a cute kid.

RICO   Don't start in on school again.

ALICE   No. You've been to school. Do you like my skirt?

RICO   No. You look like shit. Get the money before I lose my temper.

ALICE   You shouldn't come to call dressed like that. I greet you in finery, and you wear a tee shirt.

RICO   Finery? Ha!

ALICE   Be kind. Indulge me.

RICO   Fuck you.

ALICE   You like my china.

RICO   You should have stayed in South America.

ALICE   I didn't like the jungle.

RICO   I thought you said snow.

ALICE   Perhaps I didn't like the snow.

RICO   Maybe. Like I don't like you.

ALICE   My father left me that couch. In his will. It's very old.

RICO   Yeah?
   (*He stabs the couch with his knife*)

ALICE   There is hay inside. I told you. My father lives in Uruguay.

RICO   Good for him. Get the money.

ALICE   That's South American hay. It's softer than here. They grow it on the pampas. But you don't know what pampas are.

RICO   Fields.

ALICE   Yes. You have been to school.

RICO   You can get the money or you can get killed and I'll get the money. Choose.

ALICE   No. You'll have to wait.

RICO   Lady.

ALICE   My name is Alice, you strapping little pimple.

RICO   Alice.

ALICE   Can I get you another beer? Why don't you sit down? Relax, why not? This is a living room.

RICO   (*Sits*)   It's a shithole.

ALICE   You look good in this room. Like you belong.

RICO   Shut up.

ALICE   You'll get used to it after you move in.

RICO   I'm not. Shut up.

ALICE   You're even getting used to it now. You'll like the neighbors.

RICO   Neighbors?

ALICE   There's a nice old man across the hall.

RICO   He's deaf.

ALICE   I know. That doesn't mean he can't be nice.

RICO   Get the money.

ALICE   Let's look for it together.

RICO   You start. And you better get warm fast.

ALICE   You liked that game.

RICO   I hate games.

ALICE   Oh yes. You don't play baseball.

RICO   I want that money.

ALICE   You really do. I told you I'd lend you some. What do you want, to fix some girl? Or don't you go in for that . . .

RICO   Shut up.

ALICE   It's none of my business.

RICO   Right.

ALICE   Can I get you a beer? You didn't drink the last one.

RICO   No.

ALICE   You'll be expensive to keep. You waste food.

RICO   You're wasting time.

ALICE   Passing time. I get so few callers. The banks are closed.

RICO   What's that got to do with it?

ALICE   I've traveled and I'm older than you. Still, you're a nice-looking boy. I'll decide what things have to do.

RICO   Find the cash. Then decide.

ALICE   Will you knife me if I turn my back?

RICO   Take your chances.

ALICE   You were awfully noisy coming in. Did you break the lock?

RICO   I don't know.

ALICE I'll have to call a repairman before we go out to dinner. This is a rough neighborhood.

RICO We're not going to dinner.

ALICE Yes. To celebrate. You're moving in.

RICO No.

ALICE There's a window in the other room. You can stay there.

RICO Get the money and I'll leave. Make a move to leave and I'll kill you. Now get the money.

ALICE You have to do a little work. You're the thief.

RICO And you got the fat mouth.

ALICE Be nice. I wish your mother knew you were here.

RICO Shut up.

ALICE Coffee perhaps?

RICO The money.

ALICE Pushy pimple. You could ruin my business.

RICO Yeah? What business is that?

ALICE Killing children.

RICO   I wouldn't be surprised.

ALICE   You're still a child.

RICO   I'm twenty.

ALICE   Good for you. I kill children.

RICO   Am I safe?

ALICE   As you say, take your chances.

RICO   You take yours. Your one. And get the cash.

ALICE   Please.

RICO   Get it, you bitch!

ALICE   Be a nice pimple and don't make me show you how I got famous.

RICO   Get the money.

ALICE   You don't know who I am. Your mother does.

RICO   Shut up and get it.

ALICE   Push push push. That's all you say. Now why not be a nice little punk and behave. I don't think you're funny. Not a bit. You come in here, you can be nice. You don't have to be such a stinking nigger about things. I let you sit here. I let you stay. Behave. Don't push.

RICO   You talk too much.

ALICE   Your mother would know who I am. I know your mother. She should know you're here.

RICO   I have this knife, lady. It's very sharp.

ALICE   Pimple has a knife. You never saw my picture in the paper?

RICO   No.

ALICE   What made you come here?

RICO   Get the money.

ALICE   Short on cash? You didn't think I'd be home.

RICO   The money.

ALICE   I'm always home, you see. Since my picture was in the paper. I killed a child.

RICO   Shut up and get the money.

ALICE   I'm not very fond of little babies.

RICO   I can defend myself.

ALICE   But you're not a little baby. You're twenty. It was just about then.

RICO   Shut up.

ALICE   Bother you? To be in the room with me? Your mother'd know.

RICO   She hates you.

ALICE   You wet your diapers. All the time. I remember.

RICO   Then you ate them.

ALICE   And if you got scared you'd come sleep in my bed. You liked that. You were a warm child.

RICO   No.

ALICE   And during the day we'd do puzzles. You were good at them. Every week I'd buy a new puzzle. And books . . . You liked books. At school they said you were a good reader. I know.

RICO   I hate books.

ALICE   You liked these. They had pictures.

RICO   I don't know who you are.

ALICE   I'm telling you. And the park, you liked the park. We'd go for walks and you'd chase the birds. Those filthy birds. I thought they'd peck your eyes out. I hoped so.

RICO   You ever been married?

ALICE   Even the birds hated you. You were so cute. All that curly black hair. Kinky. The birds hated you.

RICO   You're batts.

ALICE   But I took care of you. You were so pretty. Every-one adored you.

RICO   You're crazy. I don't even know you.

ALICE   But at night . . . if there was rain, thunder . . . you'd come right into my bed. You were a warm child. Pretty, but scared. You scared so easily. Cigarette?

RICO   No.

ALICE   You liked to have a puff of my cigarette. You were three. Even before you began school.

RICO   I went to school.

ALICE   I know. They taught you to speak. You don't know who I am?

RICO   Crazy. That's all.

ALICE   We'll see. You're a nice-looking boy. A thief. That's nothing. I don't get many callers. The banks are closed. I don't go out.

RICO   I can see why. You're batts.

ALICE   Don't say that. This apartment isn't all I've got. Someone called me that before. I've got other things. A long time ago. I've got another life. Sit down, why not? Be comfortable. You might learn something.

RICO   You're insane.

ALICE   That's unkind. Your mother'd know.

RICO   My mother's dead. I told you that. You don't listen.
I said I'd cut your throat if you don't get the cash. You
don't hear that. You don't hear anything. Now get the
money . . . find your bitch purse and give me the
money. Otherwise, you're a dead nut.

ALICE   I kill children. I killed a baby. You haven't got
the balls to do that. (RICO *steps away*) I don't get many
callers. After the murder. (RICO *turns away*) Pimple. I
hated that bastard kid. The kid didn't like me. I killed
it. (RICO *picks up a piece of pottery*) The banks are
closed. You're a nice-looking boy though. (RICO *re-
places the pottery*) Well, I'll find the money. (ALICE
exits into the bedroom. She returns) I can't find it.
Somebody stole it.

RICO   Go to your bank.

ALICE   It's closed.

RICO   Break in.

ALICE   Like you? So noisy?

RICO   Break in.

ALICE   I need a withdrawal slip.

RICO   Not if you break in. I don't have one.

ALICE   But you don't have the money. Somebody stole it before you got here. There was another kid before you.

RICO   And you'll be dead for the next one.

ALICE   Perhaps.

RICO   Not if you get the money.

ALICE   Thank you.

RICO   No.
       (ALICE *seats herself on the couch*)

ALICE   Am I attractive?

RICO   You got fat thighs.

ALICE   Like your mother.

RICO   She works out in a gym.

ALICE   I work out.

RICO   No you don't.

ALICE   I walk in the park. I used to take you for walks. I still will.

RICO   No.

ALICE You're in good shape. Strong back. Good color. Good legs. Nice mane. Like a racehorse.

RICO No.

ALICE Come sit by me.

RICO No.

ALICE You're not friendly.

RICO You're not smart. Get the money. Then we'll talk. (ALICE *produces a purse from underneath the couch*)

ALICE This?

RICO (*Sitting beside her*) Give it here.

ALICE (*Resisting*) Wait. You won't mess it up?

RICO I won't.

ALICE Here. (*She presents it to him*) It's messy.

RICO I got eyes.

ALICE You're messing it.

RICO Sorry.

ALICE You were hard coming. Feet first. Right from the first I didn't like you. I ached from your kicking.

RICO (*Absent-minded*)   Yeah?

ALICE   You wet on a nurse. Second day. I liked you better. You had a sense of humor at least.

RICO   Where's the cash?

ALICE   Keep looking. You were ugly. Quite slimy. You were a big pimple, like now. Perhaps the nurse dipped you in vaseline because you wet her, I'm not sure. They didn't like you. I didn't like you. Does anybody really like you now? I doubt it. You don't even have a gang. Can't even get a gang together.

RICO   That's right. Where's the money?

ALICE   It might be hidden. I can't remember.

RICO   It better be here.

ALICE   You're messing. Be careful. It's there. You're a nice-looking boy. I like boys. They've always interested me. Even when I was in South America—and God knows they barely qualified as human down there, let alone men—I liked boys. Like? Yes. I liked boys.

RICO (*Still absent-mindedly*)   Good for you. Where is it?

ALICE   You asked for the purse. You got it. Keep looking. You were a bastard to bring into the world. And I don't think you were really worth it, now that I get a good look. Feet first and all that. You weren't really worth it. Still you look all right. I'm just not sure what color you are.

RICO   Shut up.

ALICE   You'll never get anywhere that way.

RICO   Get the money. I have a knife.

ALICE   So I've heard. It isn't there?

RICO   No.

ALICE   Let me look. (*She takes the purse and looks*) No. It doesn't appear to be here, does it? Sorry.

RICO   That's a very bad mistake you made. I'll have to kill you.

ALICE   I'm sorry. I really am. One more chance. I've got to remember where I put all that money.

RICO   Start now. You don't have much time.

ALICE   (*Getting up*)   Where could it be . . .

RICO   You decide.

ALICE   I'm sure it's at the bank.

RICO   It's closed.

ALICE   Oh yes.

RICO   You'll stain this couch when you bleed.

ALICE   I don't bleed.

RICO   That's your problem. We'll see.

ALICE   You'll stay and watch? I knew there was a speck of good in you somewhere. You can move in.

RICO   No.

ALICE   I won't bleed for a while, so if you're going to watch you'll have to move in.

RICO   Are you looking?

ALICE   I can't take my eyes off you. Does your mother know you're here?

RICO   (*Exasperated*)   Oh, lady! Come on! What do you think this is? This ain't the circus. I have a knife. I'm going to kill you. Don't clown around any more.

ALICE   (*Sitting by him*)   What's your name, huh? Yes, you. What's your name?

RICO   Rico.

ALICE Rico? That's strange. You're not. No. You're Paul.
I know.

RICO Rico.

ALICE Whatever you say, Paul.

RICO Get the cash.

ALICE I can't remember.

RICO You better.

ALICE Wait. Maybe I do remember. (*She puts her arm
around his shoulders*) I think I do.

RICO Where? Give it.

ALICE It might be . . . yes. Here. In my skirt pocket.
Right there.

RICO Get it.

ALICE I can't. I can't reach it.

RICO Use your arm.

ALICE No. You get it. (*She directs his arm*) Baby Paul
would get candy out of my pocket when he was little.
Paul. You remember. You'd be good and you'd get
candy.

RICO   No.

ALICE   Yes. You know that's true. Don't lie. Baby Paul.

RICO   No.

ALICE   I killed Baby Paul. He didn't like me. He lied. I killed the kid. He came out feet first. I hated that bastard. He pushed me all his life. Pushed and pulled and sucked and I hated him. He came in the room once and ordered me to do something. He was six. He ordered me! That was it. Got it? It's in the pocket.

RICO   Nothing . . .

ALICE   And that was it. I sat him down on the couch and played. We played. You remember . . .

RICO   It's not here.

ALICE   Yes it is. It's not in the bank. I know. Nothing in the bank any more. I know. And while we were there . . . You remember the puzzle? You were good at puzzles. And while we were there I just . . . (*She begins to demonstrate*) put my fingers up around that tiny white neck . . . and I squeezed until that kid turned red. Paul. You tried to yell. Turned blue. Choked . . . (*She is strangling* RICO *now*) and coughed. That puzzle was all over the floor. And then—

RICO   (*He jumps up*)   Get away!
      (*He dashes to the hall and the outside door and disappears. The door slams.* ALICE *rises and moves*

*quickly to the hall and also disappears. The stage
is empty.* ALICE's *voice rises from behind the par-
tition*)

ALICE (*Offstage*)   You're such a nice-looking boy, Baby
Paul . . .
(*She begins to laugh and the sound rises until sud-
denly . . . silence. Blackout*)

THE PIG

Characters

MELL:

A girl dressed in men's casual clothing.

CYNTHIA:

A girl dressed in a man's business suit.

MICHAEL:

A man dressed almost identically to CYNTHIA.

The setting is a rather sterile living room in an apartment. MELL *sits smoking. She wears tie-up shoes, corduroy pants, a bandana at the neck, and a man's sport coat. In all, she looks like a man dressed for the country, though she is obviously a "she."*

MELL I'll give you three to get out here. (*Pause*) One ... two ... (CYNTHIA *appears dressed impeccably in a man's gray business suit with tie, handkerchief, everything that is proper. Strangely, the suit fits quite well, and is not ridiculous on her*) You think that's funny, don't you? You crash into somebody else's house and put on his suits and jaunt about and think it's funny, don't you?

CYNTHIA I need a brief case.

MELL A brief case?

CYNTHIA I think, don't you? All of them carry brief cases. With my initials on the side, don't you think?

MELL All of who?

CYNTHIA All the businessmen. Those people. They feel naked without a brief case, I think.

MELL Come here.

CYNTHIA Don't do anything.

MELL Just come here. (CYNTHIA *does.* MELL *fiddles with the suit as a tailor might*) That's something. Look at that. Shoulders are right. Length is right. Everything perfect.

CYNTHIA I know.

MELL And you've got nothing. I like that. Nothing.

CYNTHIA Nothing what?

MELL No tit. No bazoom, honey. That's what I like.

CYNTHIA I have.

MELL I can't see it. I can't see any bulge. But I'll take your word for it. That's really sweet. No tit.

CYNTHIA Yes! You know that. That's no way to talk. You know damn well I've got one.

MELL One.

CYNTHIA Two, damn it! Two breasts. I'll show you.

MELL I believe you. Don't get upset, I'm only kidding.

CYNTHIA It's not funny.

MELL (*Mocking*) It's not funny.

CYNTHIA It isn't! Just lay off my tits or I'll have a few words for you, Mell. I don't like that joke.

MELL I won't mention your bazooms again, sweetie.

CYNTHIA Good.

MELL Come here. I want to check something.

CYNTHIA I mean, you're no movie queen yourself. If you were a big bombshell, maybe then you could talk, but you aren't. You're pretty flat yourself.

MELL All right! (*She pauses*) Come here. I want to check something. We want to be all pretty for Michael, don't we?

CYNTHIA Yes.

MELL Then come here. There's something wrong with the pants.

CYNTHIA There's nothing wrong with the pants. Everything's perfect.

MELL They're baggy! Like sacks. Your legs are too skinny.

CYNTHIA Lie!
      (*There is a pause*)

141

MELL   Your legs are beautiful. I'd give anything in the world to have just one of my legs look like yours. The other could stay the way it is, but if I had one like yours, I'd be happy. I'd be ecstatic. You've got lovely legs. Now come here, the pants are wrong.

CYNTHIA   I'll check in the mirror.
(CYNTHIA *exits into the bedroom*)

MELL   Well?

CYNTHIA (*Offstage*)   Wait a minute.

MELL   Jesus. (CYNTHIA *returns*) Well?

CYNTHIA   They're lovely.

MELL   Is that so?

CYNTHIA   Yes. The whole effect is very dapper.

MELL   The crotch sags, sweetie.

CYNTHIA   What do you mean!

MELL   You heard me. The crotch is floppy. Come here.

CYNTHIA   Oh no you don't. None of your funny stuff. We're here on business and no funny stuff. I mean that.

MELL   The crotch sags! There's no funny stuff about that! You and that goddam funny stuff. What do you think I'll do? You want to look nice for Michael, don't you?

142

CYNTHIA   I look nice already.

MELL   Fine. Forget the crotch. Forget the suit. Forget
everything. But try to grow up, all right?

CYNTHIA   I'm grown up.

MELL   Good for you.

CYNTHIA   And I've got a good chest!

MELL   Fine.

CYNTHIA   You didn't say that before. You said I was flat.

MELL   Wonderful.

CYNTHIA   That's right. It's wonderful.

MELL   Light my cigarette.

CYNTHIA   Come on, Mell. What do you mean?

MELL   I said light my cigarette.

CYNTHIA   I don't think so. You can do it yourself.

MELL   You're some gentleman.

CYNTHIA   (*Tossing a lighter*)   Here. Light it yourself.

MELL   No.

143

CYNTHIA   If you want to smoke, light your cigarette. It won't work without a light, you know.

MELL   No.

CYNTHIA   What's this "no" stuff? Light it.
      (*There is a pause*)

MELL   No. You do it. You're the gentleman. You're being rude. And stupid. And juvenile. If you're a gentleman, you'll light the cigarette without another word. Now do it! (*She pauses*) Light the butt, sweetie. I mean it.

CYNTHIA   Boy oh boy . . .

MELL   Cut the boy-oh-boys and light it.

CYNTHIA   You just push me around like nothing.

MELL   One . . . two . . .
      (CYNTHIA *grabs the lighter and holds out the flame*)

CYNTHIA   Here.
      (*A pause.* MELL *blows out the flame*)

MELL   No thanks. I don't smoke.
      (MELL *rises and goes into the bedroom.* CYNTHIA *sits. A pause*)

CYNTHIA   That was mean.

144

MELL (*Mocking, offstage*)   That was mean.

CYNTHIA   It was!

MELL   I heard you the first time, sweetie.
(*A pause*)

CYNTHIA   What're you doing?

MELL   Joining the party.

CYNTHIA   Well, it's in here. Not in the bedroom. The party's in here.

MELL   Is it?

CYNTHIA   You really get funny sometimes.

MELL (*Still offstage*)   A laugh a minute, right?

CYNTHIA   ·A million laughs.
(MELL *reappears with a hat on*)

MELL   Catch this number.

CYNTHIA   Take that off.

MELL   It's nice.

CYNTHIA   Take it off! You look stupid in that hat. You look like a gangster.

MELL   I am a gangster. Where's he keep the cigars?

CYNTHIA   What!

MELL   The cigars, Harry. Where's he keep the stoggies?

CYNTHIA   He doesn't smoke cigars.

MELL   Oh. Well, here's the hat. It'll look better on you. It'll go with the suit.

CYNTHIA   Good idea.

MELL   Put it on.

CYNTHIA   (*Toying with the hat*)   I don't think so. Not in the house. A gentleman never wears a hat inside. Didn't you know that?

MELL   I forgot.

CYNTHIA   You can't forget stuff like that. (*She pauses*) It's a pretty nice hat.

MELL   Put it on.
        (*There is a pause*)

CYNTHIA   (*Putting it on*)   There. (*A pause. She takes it off, puts it on the floor and crushes it*) I don't like it.

MELL   Good for you.
        (*A pause.* MICHAEL *enters. He wears a suit almost identical to* CYNTHIA's. *He carries a brief case. Without looking* CYNTHIA *jumps nervously*)

CYNTHIA   Oh! You scared me!
   (MICHAEL *stops, looks at the two. He goes into the
   bedroom. He returns without the case and stands*)

MICHAEL   Well?

CYNTHIA   You scared me. Really. You can't come in like
   that.
   (*A pause. She rises and goes to* MICHAEL; *she kisses
   him gently*)

MICHAEL   I'm home.

MELL   We came to see you about your pig.
   (*There is a pause*)

CYNTHIA   Relax. Come sit. I'm not scared any more.

MICHAEL   Yes.

MELL   Can Cynthia dear get you anything, Michael? A
   drink, the paper, your slippers?

CYNTHIA   Come sit.
   (MELL *rises as the two approach. As* MICHAEL *nears
   she throws the first of a series of mock punches to
   the stomach. He is properly surprised*)

MELL   Welcome home.

CYNTHIA   Stop it.
   (*A pause.* MICHAEL *sits*)

147

MICHAEL (*Relaxing*) Which one's cooking dinner? Which one of you two?

CYNTHIA You're not hungry.

MICHAEL I just asked.

MELL I'm not hungry.

CYNTHIA Just sit. Don't worry about dinner now.

MELL This is a surprise, isn't it?

CYNTHIA How do you like my new dress?

MELL Suit.

CYNTHIA Dress, Mell.

MICHAEL I recognize it, don't I? It fits quite well. It's quite becoming.

CYNTHIA I think so. (*She pauses*) I thought you'd be pleased. I got it to wear for you. I knew you'd like it.

MICHAEL But you're not cooking. I'm home, you know.

CYNTHIA We're not your wife! I mean, there's no food, Michael, and you're not hungry. You really can't be hungry. We came for a party. We came to see you. You can't really be hungry.

MICHAEL I just asked.

MELL She's not your wife.

CYNTHIA Mell!

MICHAEL It's lovely.

CYNTHIA What?

MICHAEL The dress. It's lovely.

CYNTHIA Yes. It's for you.

MICHAEL It's got a nice accent.

CYNTHIA Mell says I have a flat chest. She says that shows in this. Isn't that right, Mell?

MICHAEL Mell should know. You know, don't you, Mell?

MELL Sure.

CYNTHIA But she's wrong. I've got a nice bosom.

MICHAEL I suppose.

MELL You bulge, dear. That's your problem. (MICHAEL *rises and returns with a paper. He reads*) Nice day at the office, Michael? Hard day at the office? Make lots of money? Meet lots of people? Have lunch out. Have lunch in. Bought this. Sold that. Had a lovely time. I

never know about the office, Michael. (*She pauses*)
Nobody's sure about you at the office. What with lunch
in or lunch out. Can I get you a drink?
(*She feints another punch. A pause*)

MICHAEL   No thank you.

MELL   I wanted to help.

MICHAEL   There's nothing to help.

MELL   We came over to help. I was told help was needed
here. You needed things.

MICHAEL   No.

MELL   And I can cook. I do steak. I do peas. I do almost
anything. I can cook whatever you want.

MICHAEL   There's nothing here and I'm not hungry.

MELL   I can cook all that with no problem.
(*A pause*)

CYNTHIA   Come on, Mell. Can't you see he's tired? He's
just home from the office, and we surprised him. He
has a full life.

MELL   Did we do that?

CYNTHIA   He's in a rotten mood. Maybe we should go.

MELL   No. Then we should stay. (*She pauses*) I make all my own clothes too.

MICHAEL   There's a strange little tailor across the street. You can get a job.

MELL   Too much to do.

MICHAEL   All right.
   (MELL *goes behind* MICHAEL *and kisses him gently*)

MELL   Feel better now?

CYNTHIA   You shouldn't do that, Mell. You just can't go kissing everybody around. You can't drag me in here and then start kissing Michael while he's sitting there. It's not right. And it's not funny. You ought to stop that. (*She pauses*) I mean, she says let's go over to see Michael, and then she starts kissing you. I should kiss you if anybody does.

MICHAEL   Should you?

CYNTHIA   Yes.

MELL   Go ahead then.
   (*There is a pause*)

CYNTHIA   (*To* MICHAEL)   You're in a lousy mood, aren't you? I mean, you really get stinky sometimes.

MICHAEL   Sorry.

MELL   You can't be lovely every day. Once in a while you've got to break down. So Michael gets stinky.

MICHAEL   I'm not stinky!

CYNTHIA   Look at that rise! Boy, do you jump! That's beautiful!

MELL (*Mocking*)   That's beautiful.
(*She feints a punch at* CYNTHIA)

MICHAEL   What's that for?

MELL   For fun.

MICHAEL   It's not fun. You ought to stop that. It's not funny.

CYNTHIA   Mell just does that sometimes. She just hauls off and fakes a punch to the gut. It's terrible. I always jump.

MELL   Your gut jumps. When it's not doing something else. You ought to keep your gut to yourself. You can't share your gut.
(*There is a pause*)

CYNTHIA (*With a vengeance*)   All right! I'm cooking! There's got to be something! I'll cook whatever I get my hands on!
(*She storms out*)

MELL (*After*)   Cook your gut.

MICHAEL   You can be quite appealing at times, can't you? You appeal to me.

MELL   Do I?

MICHAEL   Yes. This is my home. I live here.

MELL   And you've got guests.

MICHAEL   You can help me build a fire.

MELL   No fireplace.

MICHAEL   I think we need a fire here. For sitting around the fire.

MELL   In the kitchen, doll. There's a fire in the kitchen. I suppose you go out on weekends and chop wood for the stove.

MICHAEL   Chop down trees. Yes.

MELL   I used to do that kind of thing. Woodsy things. I'm very capable in the great outdoors.

MICHAEL   Are you?

MELL   I am.
        (*A pause.* CYNTHIA *returns*)

CYNTHIA I can't do it. There's no food. I can't even find any matches for the stove. Why don't you get some food in this place sometime?

MICHAEL Nobody cooks.

CYNTHIA Well, somebody ought to learn. It's a mess out there. Everything in the icebox is rotten.

MELL Just heat it up, dear. Nobody wants to know.

CYNTHIA I will not! That's terrible. We could all get sick and die. You can get all kinds of awful things eating rotten food, Mell. (*She pauses*) And besides, I can't cook.

MELL Go cook.

CYNTHIA There's no food!

MICHAEL I said that before, didn't I? I said I'm not hungry, I just want a fire.

MELL We could roast a pig.

MICHAEL Yes. We could do that, couldn't we? That might be interesting. Have you got one?

MELL (*Feinting a punch to* MICHAEL) Yes! (*She pauses*) I swing a very mean axe.

CYNTHIA   Oh, Mell! Not a woodsman story.

MELL   What about woodsmen?

CYNTHIA   It's just the stories . . . hurrah for the open spaces! Hurrah for the woods! Hurrah for Mell the Outdoorsman!
(*A silence.* CYNTHIA *sits right down*)

MELL   Where's the cigars, sweetie?

MICHAEL   What?

MELL   Come on. Break out the cigars. I need a smoke.

MICHAEL   I don't have any cigars.

MELL   I like a good cigar every once in a while. It clears out my insides.

MICHAEL   Well, there aren't any.

MELL   I'll find one. (*She moves around looking for a cigar in drawers, etc.*) You haven't got one damn cigar in the whole joint . . . Wait a minute. (*She pauses*) You liar.

MICHAEL   What?

MELL (*Producing a cigar*)   See this?

MICHAEL   It isn't mine.

MELL   It isn't mine either.

MICHAEL   You pulled it out of your pocket. (*He pauses*) I don't have cigars.

MELL (*Tossing it*)   Here. Take a look. See for yourself. A stogy.

MICHAEL   It's not mine. I've never seen it before. (*He pauses*) I'd offer you a cigar, but I haven't got any. (*He pauses again*) If I had a cigar though, it'd be yours. (*He holds out the cigar*) But I don't have one.
   (MELL *takes the cigar. Another pause*)

MELL   That's too bad. I could have used a smoke right now. (*She breaks the cigar in two*) That's really too bad.
   (*There is a pause*)

CYNTHIA   For God's sake behave, Mell.

MELL   On your feet!

CYNTHIA   Yes ma'am.
   (*She stands, mocking*)

MELL   Yes *sir*!

CYNTHIA   Yes *sir*!

MELL   Suck in your gut!
    (CYNTHIA *sits right back down*)

CYNTHIA   Goddammit, Mell, cut this out. It isn't funny.

MELL   Get on your feet. On your feet!

CYNTHIA   Michael . . .

MELL   Stand!

CYNTHIA   Michael, make her stop.

MELL   One . . . two . . . (CYNTHIA *stands*) Good. Now
  suck in your gut. You're getting fat.

CYNTHIA   No!

MELL   In! (*She pauses*) Now, where'd you get that suit?

CYNTHIA   What?

MELL   Where?

CYNTHIA   In a store. I got it in a lovely store downtown.

MELL   No. Where?

CYNTHIA   I told you.

MELL   You told me wrong. Where?

CYNTHIA   Right here, goddammit!

MELL   Where here?

CYNTHIA   In the closet.

MELL   Why?

CYNTHIA   For fun. Because it was fun!
        (*There is a pause*)

MELL   Suck in your gut! Your crotch sags, sweetie, you
    know that?

CYNTHIA   No!

MELL   It sags. And the front's baggy. Where's your
    chest? You look like a pig.

MICHAEL   What?

MELL   Answer me.

CYNTHIA   Where it always is. Right here!
        (MELL *fakes a punch to* CYNTHIA)

MELL   No. That's not it. Where's your crotch?

CYNTHIA   Oh, for Christ's sake.

MELL   For your own sake. (MELL *fakes another punch*) Suck in your gut! (*She pauses*) What have you got in there, sweetie? What do you keep in that gut?

CYNTHIA   Nothing.

MICHAEL   What is this?

MELL   I don't believe that. It has to be something. Guts don't just hang out for no reason at all. They hang out because there's something inside. What is it?

CYNTHIA   Nothing! (*She pauses*) I eat too much.

MELL   There's no food in this place. You didn't cook. You can't eat too much. What is it? (MELL *fakes another punch*) What is it!

CYNTHIA   I don't know.

MELL   You can't not know. It's your gut. You're not stupid, sweetie.

CYNTHIA   I don't know!

MELL   You do. Just shout it out. Just shout out what's in there.

CYNTHIA   Michael! (MELL *punches* CYNTHIA *very hard in the stomach. She falls to the floor, doubled up. As she is hit she cries*) The pig!
    (*A long pause.* CYNTHIA *lies absolutely still on the floor.* MELL *turns to* MICHAEL)

159

MELL   You . . . (*She pauses*) You!

MICHAEL   What is it?

MELL   You . . .

MICHAEL   It couldn't be.

MELL   It could. It's your pig.

MICHAEL   No . . . I . . . listen! No! I don't need that. I
    don't need a pig! (*He pauses*) You see, I have my office,
    and my home, and my car, and a stove. I go away on
    weekends. I live alone. I don't need a pig!

MELL   Yes.

MICHAEL   I have friends. You two. Everybody keeps me
    company. There's no pig!

MELL   (*To inert* CYNTHIA)   Tell him what you told me.
    Just speak up and tell him. (*She pauses*) I said speak
    up!
        (*There is a pause*)

MICHAEL   She's out. We ought to do something.

MELL   You heard what she said.

MICHAEL   Nothing.

MELL   She said "Michael!"
        (*There is a pause*)

MICHAEL   What is it!

MELL   Your pig.

MICHAEL   She's wrong!

MELL   Is that right, sweetie? (*She pauses*) I don't think
so.

MICHAEL   What do you think I am?

MELL   A rapist.

MICHAEL   No!

MELL   What then? (*She pauses*) It's too bad you made
me break that cigar, Michael. I could really use a cigar
right now. You and your goddam crap. I had that cigar
in my hand. I wanted it.

MICHAEL   I didn't touch you.

MELL   You've done your damage.

MICHAEL   There's no damage.

MELL   Do you know that? Are you sure?

MICHAEL   Of course.

MELL   You don't know anything. (*She pauses*) You've just come from the office.

MICHAEL   I have.

MELL   It's a busy thing, an office. You've got to watch yourself.

MICHAEL   I do.

MELL   You need to relax. I know.
(*There is a pause*)

MICHAEL   I have to. I've been at the office. I'm relaxed.

MELL   Good for you. (*She pauses.* MELL *feints a gentle punch to* MICHAEL. *They laugh quietly, actually amused*) That's a lovely suit she's got on.

MICHAEL   Yes. It is.

MELL   But it doesn't fit right. If you've got a good suit, it's got to fit right or it looks wrong.

MICHAEL   Yes.

MELL   And that one doesn't. It's wrong between the legs. It needs to be taken in. It needs to fit better.

MICHAEL   She could find a tailor.

MELL   She sews herself.

MICHAEL   Then she can do it at home. It's nicer that way. There's a certain pride in a suit you've adjusted yourself.

MELL   She does that. She cuts them down and sews them back up herself. It's impressive. It's exciting. And then she has that pride in her suit.

MICHAEL   She's quite a girl. (*He pauses*) It's a very nice gray, don't you think?

MELL   But the chest is wrong. There's no accent.

MICHAEL   She's got no chest.

MELL   She could be worse. But the suit needs fixing. It needs to stick out more.

MICHAEL   Accent.

MELL   Yes. Well, I don't have that problem myself. I have a good bit of accent.

MICHAEL   Do you?

MELL   Yes. But I haven't got a suit. I've got the equipment but not the chintz. She's got the chintz and nothing to show.

MICHAEL   She's got a little chest.

MELL   Still it's practically nothing. It's inconsequential. You wouldn't even notice in a crowd. That's why the suit needs fixing. If the suit were cut right then she could go out in crowds and not worry about people talking. About people making dirty little cracks behind her back. She worries about that.

MICHAEL   Yes.

MELL   But I don't. I *know* what they say.

MICHAEL   You must be happy.

MELL   I am. I tell her about crowds, but she's not interested. She thinks crowds are silly. She's embarrassed.

MICHAEL   She'll grow out of that.

MELL   She'll get a new bra.
         (*There is a pause*)

MICHAEL   You might find a suit lying around here somewhere. Then you'd be set.

MELL   I would.

MICHAEL   You might look out there. You might find something on the rack.

MELL   Yes. I'll look then.

MICHAEL   Do. Tell me what you get.

MELL   You'll wait here?

MICHAEL   Of course. I'm interested.

MELL   I'll do it then.

MICHAEL   Do.
(*There is a pause.* MELL *moves to the bedroom.
She stops at the door*)

MELL   You'll be here?

MICHAEL   Oh yes. No question.

MELL   Good.
(*She disappears. There is a pause.* MICHAEL *lights*
a cigarette)

MICHAEL   I'm still here.

MELL   I hear you . . .

MICHAEL   Have you got anything?

MELL   I just started. (*She pauses.* MICHAEL *smiles gently*)
There's an awful lot of crap, you know. (*She pauses
again*) Wait a minute.

165

MICHAEL   I'm still here.

MELL   I said wait a minute. I know you're there . . . I've got one. I think this does it.

MICHAEL   What about the accent?

MELL   Very good. But there's one thing. You've got to help.

MICHAEL   How's the accent?

MELL   You'll see! Now get in here and help. I'm stuck.
(MICHAEL *stubs out his cigarette and rises*)

MICHAEL   I'm coming in there.

MELL   I told you to! Now get in here!
(MICHAEL *exits to the bedroom*)

MICHAEL (*Offstage*)   Now that's something . . . (*There is a very loud slap*) Oh!
(*The lights fade fast on* CYNTHIA *on the floor. The lights come up.* CYNTHIA *is sitting, and there is moving about in the other room.* MICHAEL *appears, tucking in his shirt and doing his tie. He ignores* CYNTHIA. *There is a pause*)

CYNTHIA   I'm bored . . . I said I'm bored! This is your place, isn't it! . . . It's a damn bore, really. Just a lot of sitting around . . . You're a mess. You look terrible.

MICHAEL Do I?

CYNTHIA You do. I can tell you that. You look lousy.

MICHAEL I had a hard day at the office.

CYNTHIA You think you work too hard, don't you? You just sit around. You don't go out and do business. You sit around and do business. And then you get tired. I don't understand that. (*She pauses*) I'm hungry.

MICHAEL There's the kitchen . . .

CYNTHIA Why don't you whip up dinner? Roast a pig.

MICHAEL No!

CYNTHIA I want to eat.

MICHAEL There's no pig.
(MELL *enters. She wears a gray suit like the others and is also re-dressing. She ignores* CYNTHIA)

CYNTHIA Where have you been?

MELL Out.

CYNTHIA Oh, come on. Where have you been? I'm sitting around here waiting for dinner, waiting to have a decent conversation, and everybody goes out. Now they come back. Then you'll probably go out again. What is this?

MELL (*To* MICHAEL) You've got a very hard edge today, sweetie. You ought to do something about that. You work too hard.

MICHAEL I don't think so.

MELL Well, you do.

CYNTHIA What the hell's a hard edge?

MELL You better get rid of it.

CYNTHIA What is it?

MELL (*To* CYNTHIA) Look, Harry, can't you behave? Don't ask questions.

CYNTHIA Then you shut up about this hard-edge business. (*She pauses*) I'm still hungry.
        (*There is another pause*)

MELL Michael, dear . . .

MICHAEL What?

MELL Don't say "what." Say "what *dear*."

MICHAEL What?
        (*There is a pause*)

MELL I think you ought to know something.

MICHAEL What?

CYNTHIA You've got a hard edge today.
 (*There is a pause*)

MELL I don't like getting dragged into someone's bedroom and finding another girl's clothes all over the
place. It's rude. (*She pauses*) Well . . . you know what
I'm talking about. Explain that tiny bra and those
teensy underpants on the floor. What about them?

CYNTHIA It's not a tiny bra!

MELL What about it? Nobody likes to be second, you
know.

MICHAEL They're mine.

MELL Oh.

MICHAEL I keep them around. For the hell of it. That's
my stuff on the floor. You've got to have everything
these days.

CYNTHIA You know damn well it's my stuff. And it's not
tiny.

MELL Who lives here?

CYNTHIA Michael.

MELL   Then he should know, shouldn't he? It's his home.

MICHAEL   It's mine.
(*There is a pause*)

CYNTHIA   You really do a fine job, Michael.

MICHAEL   What?

CYNTHIA   A fine job. You handle everything very well. It's impressive, and it's a pleasure.

MELL   What is?

CYNTHIA   You know.

MELL   I do not.

CYNTHIA   In bed. You know that.

MICHAEL   No!

CYNTHIA   You've forgotten already.

MICHAEL   I haven't.

CYNTHIA   Then you know how you were in bed.

MELL   In bed?

CYNTHIA   Just now.

MELL   Michael! What did you do?

MICHAEL   Nothing.

MELL   Michael!

CYNTHIA   You better not lie.

MELL   You dragged her off in your bedroom while I was out?

MICHAEL   I didn't.

CYNTHIA   Sure. You didn't. I mean, you ought to see the marks, Mell. It's terrible.

MELL   You marked this poor girl.

CYNTHIA   He always does. He's sick.

MELL   There were things on that floor just now. Little nasties. You deny that?

MICHAEL   Mine.

CYNTHIA   You marked me while she was out. Deny that.

MICHAEL   I do.

CYNTHIA   Liar.

MELL   You're a sick boy.

CYNTHIA And you haven't got any food, either. That really gets me. You have people over to dinner and then there's no pig.

MICHAEL You're not over to dinner! (*He pauses*) You crashed in. You did it all yourselves. Don't talk about pig!
(*There is a pause*)

MELL Well . . .

CYNTHIA This is something, isn't it?

MELL Get your coat. We'll go. (*She pauses*) And don't forget your bundle.

CYNTHIA What bundle?

MELL The one you came in with. The only one there is. The big bundle.

CYNTHIA I lost it.

MELL Don't say that. (*She pauses*) And get your bundle.

CYNTHIA I'll get my coat because that's all I have.

MELL (*Moving around*) Then I'll get your bundle. It's around here somewhere. (*She looks in drawers, under things, etc.*) You always dump it somewhere, don't you?

CYNTHIA I do not.

MELL   You do. It's not in here; it must be in the bedroom. You were in the bedroom, weren't you?

CYNTHIA   Certainly not.

MELL   Liar. (*She disappears into the bedroom. She returns almost immediately*) It's not in there either.

CYNTHIA   There isn't anything.

MELL   You're sure you haven't got it?
        (MELL *fakes a punch to* CYNTHIA. CYNTHIA *doesn't even flinch*)

CYNTHIA   No.

MELL   Good for you. Michael . . . where is it?

MICHAEL   What?

MELL   The bundle, baby.

MICHAEL   I don't know what you're talking about.

MELL   Don't you?

CYNTHIA   You're sure?

MICHAEL   I don't.
        (MELL *reaches in a drawer and produces a lifesize rubber baby doll*)

MELL   What about this? (*She pauses*) It's not mine.

MICHAEL   Put that away!

CYNTHIA   It's not mine either.

MICHAEL   Put it away!
       (*There is a pause*)

CYNTHIA   Put *what* away?

MICHAEL   That thing.

MELL   What thing?

MICHAEL   *That* thing!

CYNTHIA   What's it called? (*She pauses*) Name it.
       (*There is another pause*)

MELL   The pig.

MICHAEL   Get out! And take your thing with you!

CYNTHIA   Our thing? It's not my thing. I left my pig somewhere else. I misplaced it somewhere.

MELL   It's not my pig. I'm safe. I smoke cigars. Get the coats. (CYNTHIA *disappears quickly and returns with her coat and* MELL's) Thank you.
       (*They put their coats on over their suits, each carefully holding the doll for the other. There is a pause*)

174

MELL   Well, what about the pig, Michael?

CYNTHIA   It isn't mine.

MELL   Or mine.

CYNTHIA   So it must be yours. Unless somebody left it here by mistake.

MICHAEL   No!

MELL   (*In a rage*)   Well, whose is it then! It's got to be somebody's! They don't just appear! (*As she delivers the next line she raises the doll above her head and smashes it down hard on the table for exclamation. The doll squeaks*) They don't just show up!
   (*The doll lies on the table. There is dead silence*)

CYNTHIA   Oh no . . . (MICHAEL *reaches a hand toward the "dead" doll*) Oh no, Michael . . .

MELL   We've got to go. I can't stay any longer.

CYNTHIA   Michael, you bastard. Look what you did to your own pig. You killed the dirty little pig.

MELL   What a mess.

CYNTHIA   You smashed that skull to smithereens, Michael.

MELL   I can't stay any more. (*She goes to exit, then stops*)
Come on, Harry. (CYNTHIA *backs away in horror*) We'll
call the police.
(MELL *disappears.* CYNTHIA *is still backing away*)

CYNTHIA   Boy oh boy.
(*She too disappears. The door shuts quietly.*
MICHAEL *is left sitting. He picks up the doll and
puts it back down. Silence. He reaches for it again.
There is a loud knock-knock-knock on the door*)

Blackout

About the Author

DAVID TRAINER was born in West Hartford, Connecticut, in 1947; he attended the University of Pennsylvania in Philadelphia for a little over a year, and now lives in New York City. Two of his early plays, *Not Like Connecticut* and *Demonstration*, were presented by the Lake George Summer Theater Project in the summer of 1967. He is a member of the Playwrights Unit, where *The Undertaking* was first performed in April, 1968.